Collector's Encyclopedia Of

R.S. Prussia

FOURTH SERIES

FEATURING:
R.S., E.S., O.S., & C.S. PORCELAIN

Mary Frank Gaston

COLLECTOR BOOKS
A Division of Schroeder Publishing Co., Inc.

The current values in this book should be used only as a guide. They are not intended to set prices, which vary from one section of the country to another. Auction prices as well as dealer prices vary greatly and are affected by condition as well as demand. Neither the Author nor the Publisher assumes responsibility for any losses that might be incurred as a result of consulting this guide.

Searching for a Publisher?

We are always looking for knowledgeable people considered to be experts within their fields. If you feel that there is a real need for a book on your collectible subject and have a large comprehensive collection, contact us.

COLLECTOR BOOKS
P.O. Box 3009
Paducah, Kentucky 42002-3009

On the Cover:
Top Right: Demi-tasse Cup, 2¼"h, and Saucer, (Plate 155).
Top Left: Chocolate Pot, 9½"h, (Plate 186).
Middle Right: Teapot, 6"h, (Plate 127).
Middle: Covered Sugar Bowl, 5"h, (Plate 126).
Bottom Left: Plate, 11"d, (Plate 73).
Bottom Right: Covered Butter Dish, 5"h; Underplate, 7½"d, (Plate 50).

Cover design: Beth Summers
Book design: Michelle Dowling

Additional copies of this book may be ordered from:

Collector Books
P.O. Box 3009
Paducah, KY 42002-3009
or
Mary Frank Gaston
P.O. Box 342
Bryan, TX 77806

@$24.95. Add $2.00 for postage and handling.

Copyright: Mary Frank Gaston, 1995
Updated Values: 1997

Contents

Acknowledgments

For this *Fourth Series* of *The Collector's Encyclopedia of R.S. Prussia, Featuring R.S., E.S., O.S., and C.S. Porcelain*, I extend my most sincere appreciation again to all of those who contributed to the *Third Series*. When that project was begun in 1991, collectors thought they were only contributing to one book. The material and photographs, however, were too large for one volume, and as a result this *Fourth Series* was the outcome.

Special thanks once more to my editor, Lisa Stroup, and her staff, for their excellent work in shaping the material into a beautiful book. I also express my thanks again to Mr. R. H. (Ron) Capers for his help in supplying materials, photographs, and translations for these latest two books of mine on Schlegelmilch china. It is my pleasure to dedicate this *Fourth Series* to him in appreciation of his dedication to the study of this exquisite porcelain and its manufacturers.

The following individuals assisted Mr. Capers in Germany:

Herr Reiner Wurzler, Director of the Suhl city and county archives

Frau Eleonore Richter, Suhl Hometown Historical Researcher

Frau Christa Anshütz, Suhl City Guide/Travel Leader

Herr Dr. Martin Kummer, Lord Mayor of the City of Suhl

Herr Dr. Gerhard Soppa from Kreis Falkenberg, scholar of Tillowitz and the R.S. Factory

Herr u. Frau Bösling (Werner & Rosi) from Hamburg, collectors

Herr Dr. Dietrich W. Hahlbrock from Hamburg, husband of the late Brigitte (Koch) Hahlbrock, the last Schlegelmilch family owner of the Reinhold Schlegelmilch Porzellanfabrik, Tillowitz, Upper Silesia

Mr. John Maltman, photographer for Mr. Capers' collection

Contributors of Photographs for the *Fourth Series:*

Martha and Robert R. Allen, Manns Harbor, NC
Charles and Karen Aschenbeck, Houston, TX
Helen Bailey, Kirksville, MO
Lawrence and Judith Bazaar
John Becker, Columbus, OH
John and Bea Bell
Rose Ellen and Walt Beyer, Omaha, NE
Edda Biesterfeld, Bonn, Germany
Merle N. Blanton, Mechanicsburg, OH
Phyllis Boege, Richton Park, IL
Kerry and Christine Bottcher, Bowmanstown, PA
Dale R. Bowser, Brookville, OH
Freda Bradford
Harold and Barbara Bragg, OH
Noreen and R.H. Capers, Fort Meade, MD
Suzan Cartwright
Richard and Florence Chaney, Myrtle Creek, OR
Nancy J. Clifford, WA
Frances and Terry Coy, Louisville, KY
Phillip Crutcher, Peru, IL
Edna M. Dennie
Mrs. Ralph Dickey, Mt. Vernon, IN
Sharon Dollos, DuQuoin, IL
Lavaine Donovan
Mike Edgar
Patty Erickson
Margie Fowler, Warrenton, MO
Ken and Debra Fuelberth, IL
Gloria and Byman Geyer, Mansfield, TX
Doris and Carl Gibbs, San Antonio, TX
Nancy Glass, Germantown, TN
John and Sharon Gold, Easton, PA
Robert Gollmar, Rochester, WI
Marian E. Gordon, OH
Nash and Jeannie Hayes, Lebanon, KY
Cynthia Helping, West Milton, OH
John and Deanna Hill, Forest City, IA
Claire Hohnstein
Peter Hohnstein and Deb Schark, Robinson, IL
Maurice and Dee Hooks, Lawrenceville, IL
Maurice L. Hooks, WA
David W. Irwin, Jr.

Nancy A. Jensen, WI
Jody's Antiques, Antique World Mall, North Little
    Rock, AR
Lee Kirkpatrick
Delbert Krug, Solon, IA
John Law, Fort Dodge, IA
Carl and Phyllis Leohr
Paul Linden, Bellville, WI
Rich and Priscilla Lindstrom, St. Joseph, IL
Debbie Lobel, Arlington, TX
Dr. and Mrs. Wm. J. Luke, Scottsdale, AZ
Mary and Robert McCaslin, Danville, IN
Clarence and Ida Meyer, Fort Scott, KS
Marlene and Gene Miller, IN
David Mullins, Columbus, OH
Hoy and Virginia Mullins, WV
Byron Murray
Robert Pompilio, Garden City, NY
Irene Reeves, Alexandria, IN
Kevin Reiman
Jean Riecker, Northville, MI
The Rileys of Ohio
Dale and Amber Rothrock
Tom Rouch, Pierston, IN
Lucille Rowoldt
Barbara and Shelby Smith, Muncie, IN
Donald South
Mr. and Mrs. Oscar Srp, Dayton, OH
Adam Stein, III, High Point, NC
Arlo Stender, Cumberland, IA
Thomas Surratt
Janelle and Gordon Sweeter
Yvonne L. Titchener
Mr. and Mrs. Gary Thomas, Alexandria, IN
Cheryl and Tim van der Hagen, MN
Judy White, Kalamazoo, MI
Joyce and Jack Williams, Irvine, CA
Bonnie and John Willis, El Dorado Hills, CA
Frank Wine, Jr., Portsmouth, VA
Pam Wolfe
Woody Auctions, Douglass, KA
Pete and Viola Zwern, Denver, CO

To Mr. R. H. (Ron) Capers

Preface

The *Fourth Series* on Schlegelmilch china focuses on porcelain made by the Reinhold Schlegelmilch factories in Suhl and Tillowitz which bears marks other than the R.S. Prussia mark. China made by the Erdmann Schlegelmilch factory in Suhl, and china made by the Oscar Schlegelmilch factory in Langewiesen are also presented in this edition. A few examples of china made by the Carl Schlegelmilch factory in Mäbendorf are also included.

Collectors are referred to the *Third Series* for a discussion of new material regarding the history of the various Schlegelmilch factories. The revised chronology of R.S. marks which was printed in the *Third Series* has been repeated here. A revised chronology of marks for the E.S. and O.S. factories is presented in this edition.

The book is divided into several sections according to factory, and each section is subdivided by particular marks. For example, the first section on Reinhold Schlegelmilch china includes separate divisions for the R.S. Suhl Marks, R.S. Steeple Marks, R.S. Germany Marks, etc. Brief discussions of a type of mark introduce each division which is followed by photographs of the mark and its variations and then by photographs of examples with those marks. All marks have been renumbered in this edition. They are numbered by specific mark, such as R.S. Suhl Marks 1, 2, 3, and R.S. Steeple Marks 1, 2, 3, and so forth.

A special section on Ambiguous Marks has been written for this *Fourth Series*. Certain marks such as embossed stars, Saxe Altenburg, Royal Vienna, and other "Royal" marks have increasingly come under the "umbrella" of Schlegelmilch china because of their shapes and decorations which often bear a striking similarity to porcelain associated with the Reinhold Schlegelmilch marks. This section has been included to point out the similarities and the differences among these various marks and the china on which they are found.

Other information which might be of interest to collectors can be found in several Appendices at the end of the book. These include R.S. Tillowitz Figurines, the Erdmann Schlegelmilch family tree, and documents from the Erdmann Schlegelmilch factory.

There is an Index for R.S. Prussia Mold Revisions. Several R.S. Prussia Mold numbers have been changed, deleted, or placed under other marks and are shown in this *Fourth Series* rather than in the *Third Series* under the R.S. Prussia mark. Other Indexes include one for Steeple Floral Decorations and one for Ambiguous Marks Decorations. There are also Indexes for objects and major decoration themes for R.S., E.S., and O.S. china. A current Value Guide lists the estimated dollar market range for pieces shown. Modern reproductions and items shown in the Appendices are not included in the Value Guide.

Reinhold Schlegelmilch Marks and Photographs

Revised Chronology of R.S. Marks
R.S. Suhl
R.S. Steeple
R.S. Germany
R.S. Tillowitz and R.S. Silesia
R.S. Wing Mark
Molded "RS" Marks
R.S. Germany Double Marks
R.S. Poland

RS Prussia Wreath Mark	circa late 1800s to shortly after World War I
RS Suhl Wreath Mark	beginning date unclear, but not before early 1900s; not used after 1917
RS Steeple Marks	circa 1895 until circa the beginning of World War I
RS Germany Marks	circa a few years prior to World War I until 1945
RS Tillowitz, Silesia Mark	circa 1920s to 1940s
RS Silesia Marks	circa 1920s to 1940s
RS Poland Mark	circa after 1945 (probably between 1947 and 1949*) to 1956
PT Poland Mark	after 1956 (and perhaps as early as 1950)*

*These dates reflect the more logical time period rather than that shown by references.

R.S. Suhl

The R.S. Suhl mark is identical to the R.S. Prussia mark, except for the word "Suhl" rather than "Prussia." The question remains unanswered as to when the R.S. Suhl mark was first initiated. In my *Second Series* (1986: 11), I discussed my reasons for disagreeing with Röntgen's date of 1904 (the same date he listed for the RSP mark) as the beginning year for the R.S. Suhl mark. Undoubtedly, the RSP mark and the R.S. Suhl mark overlap, but I doubt that they were both initiated the same year.

It might be argued that the R.S. Suhl mark was used prior to the RSP mark. The Erdmann Schlegelmilch factory used "Suhl" in its marks. Since the R.S. factory was started in Suhl after the E.S. factory, it might seem that the later company would also choose the word "Suhl" for its first marks. The majority of molds and floral decorations found on R.S. Suhl marked items, however, do not agree with that assumption. The simple shapes and stylized floral designs are those popular during the early "teen" years of the twentieth century rather than the 1870s to 1890s. In fact the Butler Bros. Catalog of 1911 shows a common RS Suhl vase mold (see Photograph 8) and describes the decoration as a "nouveau design." The floral pattern was in a stylized form. When comparing floral decorations among the different RS marks, it is quickly apparent that the designs found with the R.S. Suhl marks are much more similar to those found with R.S. Germany or R.S. Tillowitz marks than to those floral transfers found on china with the R.S. Prussia mark.

The scarce amount of items with the R.S. Suhl mark available on the American market may be attributed to a time when little Schlegelmilch china was exported to the United States. During World War I, German goods were embargoed by this country. I would suggest that time period for when the R.S. Suhl mark was mostly used. It is also interesting to note that the R.S. Suhl mark is not shown in any of the Coburg Ceramic Directories which were available for reference (see years of entries in the Bibliography).

The majority of R.S. Suhl marked china which is shown in this edition was found by Mr. Capers in Germany. This fact as well as the very small number of R.S. Suhl marked items shown in my other two books substantiates the statement that R.S. Suhl marked china is scarce in the United States.

Some of the figural themes on R.S. Suhl china are like those found with the RSP mark. The Melon Eaters is one example. Molds, such as RSP Mold 181, are found with either the RSP or R.S. Suhl mark. The "Colonial Ladies" transfers are found with the R.S. Suhl mark as well as with the RSP mark and the R.S. Steeple mark. Some of the exotic birds, such as the Crowned Crane, Hummingbird, and Parrots are found as decorations on china with either the R.S. Suhl, RSP, or R.S. Poland mark. This overlapping of marks reflects a transition in marks from one time period to another or one factory to another (Suhl or Tillowitz). The same decoration transfers were used but different marks were applied.

The R.S. Suhl mark should not have been used after 1917, when the factory moved from Suhl to Tillowitz. The exception would be, of course, if any R.S. Suhl marked stock was transferred to Tillowitz in 1917, and then exported from there.

The R.S. Suhl mark is sometimes found in conjunction with a blue elongated Beehive mark (R.S. Suhl Marks 3 and 4). A few examples with that mark are shown here. Notice that the Beehive mark also occurs with just the RS Wreath mark (without "Suhl" or "Prussia"). While one cannot attribute all Beehive marks to the R.S. factories, there is no question of attribution when the pieces are double marked with an RS Wreath or an R.S. Suhl mark. Three examples which were only marked with a Beehive have been included here because the mark is exactly like the type found with the R.S. Suhl or RS Wreath marks. The decoration is also characteristic of Schlegelmilch china.

Two other Suhl marks have been discovered which can probably be credited to the R.S. factory. One is R.S. Suhl Mark 5. That mark incorporates "R.S. Suhl" under a leafy branch. The mark was found in both red and green. The decorations on the items shown here are the same as Steeple decoration "Q" and embossed Star Mark decoration "a." The shapes are similar to Steeple marked china as are the dark backgrounds. This may have been an experimental mark.

Mark 7, "Royal Suhl, Germany," is also probably an R.S. Schlegelmilch mark. The example shown here is RSP Mold 93. It has the Mill scene decoration and Steeple background color #4. (See Steeple marked china and Ambiguous Marks.)

At the end of this section, several unmarked examples are attributed to the R.S. Suhl marks based on their molds and decorations. Mold numbers have been assigned to R.S. Suhl marked vases. Pieces which have an R.S. Suhl mark but are examples of RSP molds are described with the RSP mold number.

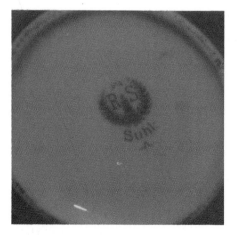

R.S. Suhl Mark 1, green and red wreath with red lettering.

R.S. Suhl Mark 2 in green.

R.S. Suhl Mark 3, like Mark 1, with elongated Blue Beehive Mark.

R.S. Suhl Mark 4, (green and red wreath with "R.S." initials in red but without either "Suhl," or "Prussia") with Blue Beehive Mark.

R.S. Suhl Mark 5, "R.S. Suhl" printed in red or green under a leafy branch with "Made in Germany" printed underneath.

R.S. Suhl Mark 6 in green with all letters capitalized.

R.S. Suhl Mark 7, "Germany Royal Suhl" printed in red.

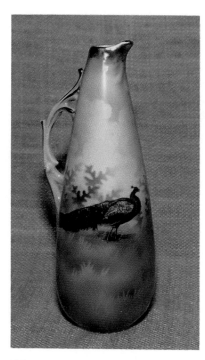

Plate 1. *One handled Dish or Bowl, 11"d, RSP Mold 181; vivid pink and red floral decor, gold trim; R.S. Suhl Mark 2 with "Handpainted" (in German).*

Plate 2. *One handled Dish or Bowl, 11"d, RSP Mold 181; white daisies on shaded green background; R.S. Suhl Mark 2.*

Plate 3. *Ewer, 7", Peacock scenic decor; unmarked (mold is the same as Plate 480 in GI); R.S. Suhl Mold 1.*

Plate 4. *Ewer, 9"h, Josephine portrait framed with a gold scrolled design; red finish on upper part of body; illegible mark; R.S. Suhl Mold 1.*

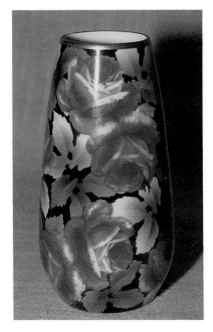

Plate 5. *Vase, 7⅛"h, dark pink roses on black background, gold trim; R.S. Suhl Mark 2; R.S. Suhl Mold 2.*

Plate 7. *Vase, 7⅛"h, white chrysanthemums on ivory shading to brown background, gold trim; R.S. Suhl Mark 2; R.S. Suhl Mold 2.*

Plate 6. *Vase, 7⅛"h, large pink lilies with large leaves on black background, gold trim; R.S. Suhl Mark 2; R.S. Suhl Mold 2.*

Plate 8. *Vase, 7"h, white roses with a light yellow tint on shaded green background; R.S. Suhl Mark 2; R.S. Suhl Mold 3.*

Plate 9. *Pair of Vases, 9"h, figural pastoral decor; gold stencilled designs over cobalt blue finish on base; gold trim. R.S. Suhl Mark 2 with initials "A.F." on each piece; R.S. Suhl Mold 3.*

Plate 10. Vase, 9¼"h, large pink and white roses on black background, gold handles; R.S. Suhl Mark 2; R.S. Suhl Mold 4.

Plate 11. Vase, 11⅝"h, stylized white poppies on ivory shading to brown background; R.S. Suhl Mark 2; R.S. Suhl Mold 5.

Plate 12. Vase, 8½"h, multicolored floral decor on ivory shading to brown background; R.S. Suhl Mark 6; R.S. Suhl Mold 5.

Plate 13. Vase, 10⅝"h; stylized pink roses; R.S. Suhl Mark 6; R.S. Suhl Mold 5.

Plate 14. *Pair of Vases, 5¼"h, large pink flowers with white snowballs accented by gold stencilled designs; R.S. Suhl Mark 2; R.S. Suhl Mold 6.*

Plate 15. *Pair of Vases, 8⅝"h, figural scenic seaside decor, unusual "back" views of figures; R.S. Suhl Mark 2; R.S. Suhl Mold 7.*

Plate 16. *Vase, 6"h, handpainted red roses with green leaves around top half of vase; decoration is underglaze; R.S. Suhl Mark 2 with "Handmalerei" (handpainted); R.S. Suhl Mold 8.*

Plate 17. *Vase, 6"h, lavender and white flowers on shaded green background; R.S. Suhl Mark 2; R.S. Suhl Mold 8.*

Plate 18. *Vase, 7⅜"h, RSP FD39, lilac clematis; R.S. Suhl Mark 1; R.S. Suhl Mold 9.*

Plate 19. *Vase, 3⅛"h x 3¼"d, salesman's sample; white roses; R.S. Suhl Mark 2; R.S. Suhl Mold 10.*

Plate 20. *Vase 6"h, figural decor of a Woman Feeding Chickens (a different transfer from the Victorian Vignettes series); R.S. Suhl Mark 1; R.S. Suhl Mold 11 (similar to RSP Mold 908 without handles, see G1).*

Plate 21. *Vase, 5"h, RSP Mold 907, large pink flowers with white snowballs on black background; R.S. Suhl Mark 2.*

Plate 22. *Cup, 1⅞"h x 2"d, and Saucer; pink roses; gold stencilled border around middle of cup and on interior rim; R.S. Suhl Mark 2 in red (rare mark).*

Plate 23. *Cup and Saucer, white floral design decorates interior of cup; R.S. Suhl Mark 2.*

16

Plate 24. Cup and Saucer, souvenir item for Copenhagen (Danish words are printed under design); R.S. Suhl Mark 1.

Plate 25. Two handled Dish, 8⅛"d, lavender and white flowers, gold trim; R.S. Suhl Mark 6.

Plate 26. Plate, 10"d, pierced handles; white roses with a yellow tint on ivory to shaded brown background; R.S. Suhl Mark 2.

Plate 28. *Covered Box or Powder Jar, 3⅝"d, stylized white flowers; R.S. Suhl Mark 2.*

Plate 27. *Covered Box or Powder Jar, 5½"d, pink roses; R.S. Suhl Mark 2.*

Plate 29. *Covered Box shaped as an Egg, 5⅞"l x 4"w x 3½"h; a dark pink and a light pink rose decorate top, gold trim; R.S. Suhl Mark 2; rare item.*

Plate 30. *Covered Box shaped as an Egg, 3¼"l x 2¼"w; light yellow roses decorate top, gold trim; R.S. Suhl Mark 2; rare item.*

Plate 31. *Vase, 8"h, Melon Eaters figural decor; red finish on most of body; gold beaded frame work and border; opalescent jewel; gold handles; R.S. Suhl Mark 3; R.S. Suhl Mold 3.*

Plate 32. *Pair of Ewers, 6¼"h, Victorian Vignettes Series: left, Lady Watering Flowers; right, Lady Feeding Chickens; heavy gold embellishments; R.S. Suhl Mark 4; RSP Mold 900.*

Plate 33. *Cup, 2⅞"h, and Saucer, souvenir item for Berlin, gold stencilled designs decorate teal blue borders; R.S. Suhl Mark 3.*

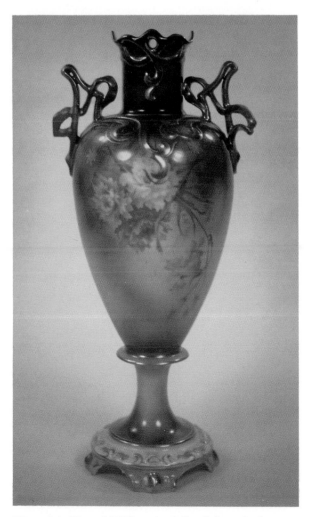

Plate 34. *Vase, 13½"h, mixed floral decor is the same as Star Mark "a" transfer (see Ambiguous Marks); dark green finish; gold trim; R.S. Suhl Mark 5 in green; R.S. Suhl Mold 12.*

Plate 35. *Vase 13"h, mixed floral decor is the same as Steeple decoration "Q" (see Steeple Marks); dark green finish; gold trim; R.S. Suhl Mark 5 in red; R.S. Suhl Mold 13.*

Plate 36. *Pair of Vases, 8½"h; Parrots and Ostriches decorate both vases (see Plate 37 for reverse side of each vase); cobalt blue finish overlaid with gold enameled designs; unmarked (mold is the same as shown in Plates 3 and 4 without handle and lip); R.S. Suhl Mold 14; unmarked.*

Plate 37. *Reverse side of Vases in Plate 36.*

Plate 38. *Bowl, 5½"d, RSP Mold 93; Mill scene with R.S. Steeple background color 4 (see R.S. Steeple section); R.S. Suhl Mark 7.*

Plate 39. *Child's Set: Tea or Coffee Pot; Covered Sugar Bowl; Cup and Saucer; figural pastoral scenic decor; cobalt blue finish; gold trim; R.S. Suhl Mark 3 (Beehive mark without R.S. Suhl wreath mark).*

Plate 40. *Vase, 9½"h, Hummingbirds; white satin finish; unmarked; R.S. Suhl Mold 3.*

Plate 41. *Vase, 10½"h, Crowned Cranes decor; unmarked; R.S. Suhl Mold 2.*

Plate 42. *Vase, 9½"h, Hummingbirds; white satin finish; unmarked.*

R.S. Steeple

The R.S. Steeple marks were used by the Tillowitz factory from about 1895 until the beginning years of World War I. The Steeple (or Church) mark is found with either the words "Prussia" or "Germany." The mark was stamped in red, green, dark blue, black, or gold. See Steeple Marks 1 through 5.

A few molds and decorations may overlap between R.S. Steeple marked china and RSP or R.S. Germany marked pieces. The Steeple marks, however, largely characterize a specific set of molds and decorations. I examined examples of unmarked china in G1 and G2 together with a large number of pictures of unmarked china. From that study, it became obvious that some molds should be re-classified based on the fact that some of the molds which had been placed under the RSP mark and given an RSP mold number were unmarked examples. While those particular molds could not be documented with an RSP mark, they were found with a Steeple mark. Therefore, I have removed some molds from the RSP classification and moved them to the Steeple section. In a few cases, such as old RSP Mold 6, an example was noted to have been found with an RSP mark (see Gaston, 1986: 37). From the overwhelming amount of unmarked pieces in that mold, however, as well as the decoration characteristics, the mold should be categorized as R.S. Steeple china rather than R.S. Prussia. Another RSP Mold, 343, is occasionally found with an RSP mark. That particular mold, however, is more often found with a Steeple mark or one of the "Ambiguous" Marks. It has been assigned a Steeple Mold number for Steeple marked examples of that mold. The RSP Mold number 343 has been maintained only for RSP marked examples of that particular mold.

Mold changes are shown here:

Old RSP Mold Number	New Steeple Mold Number
6	24
26	6
27	6
51	26
86	5
328	1

Old RSP Mold Number		New Steeple Mold Number
343	(same RSP Mold # if object has RSP Mark/Decoration)	8
402		9
514		6
520		7
615		12
863		8

Pieces with R.S. Steeple marks are shown first in the following photographs. Steeple mold numbers (ST Mold) have been listed for all marked pieces, except some of the desk accessories and novelty pieces. Flat and Vertical objects which have matching molds have been given the same mold number and are shown together. This is in contrast to how the RSP Molds are arranged. The Steeple mold numbers on marked examples range from 1 to 25.

A Floral Decoration Letter (FD) has been used to identify different floral transfers found on Steeple marked china. These particular floral designs are rarely, if ever, found with any other RS mark. The transfers are easy to distinguish from the pictures. Because the molds are arranged in numerical order, it was not possible to arrange the floral designs in alphabetical order. The Floral Decoration letters on Steeple marked china, however, range from "A" to "R."

To round out the characteristics of Steeple marked china, a background number (BG) has also been used for relevant examples. These background colors may be found only on the border of pieces or over the entire surface. They are numbered 1 through 6 and are described below:

BG1............wide brilliant gold border
BG2............cobalt blue border overlaid with white flowers
BG3............overall cobalt blue background
BG4............pink, green, and orange "glow" background
BG5............green border overlaid with white flowers
BG6............blue and purple Tiffany iridescent finish on border

This group of identifying traits (mold, floral decor, and background color) has been developed not only to show the earmarks of Steeple marked china, but also to use as a method to determine whether examples of unmarked china should be classified as Steeple china rather than R.S. Prussia china.

Following the examples of Steeple marked china are unmarked pieces which match a definite Steeple mold. These items may have one of the Steeple decorations or background colors. Some, though, have a decoration not found (or unavailable for this edition) with a Steeple mark. The decoration becomes a Steeple decoration, however, because it is on a documented Steeple mold. There are five decorations which fall under this category. Thus the Steeple Decoration letters are extended by the letters "S" through "X."

One unmarked mold which was classified as RSP Mold 51 in G1 does not match any marked Steeple mold. Examples always seem to be unmarked. That mold has been deleted from the R.S. Prussia classification. The decorations on the mold, however, are ones associated with the Steeple marks. That mold is now Steeple mold 26. Photographs of examples of the mold are shown after the other unmarked Steeple molds.

Next are pictures of several other molds which are also unmarked. These molds do match documented RSP molds. The decoration on these unmarked pieces, however, is clearly a Steeple decoration rather than one commonly found on RSP marked china. Because the items are unmarked but have a Steeple decoration, they have been placed under the Steeple examples. These molds are described with their RSP Mold numbers, but the decorations and background colors have Steeple letters and numbers respectively. The RSP molds included here are numbers 23, 29, 30, 87, 98, 339, 347, 517, 525, 657, 664. (Note that Mold 664 has replaced Mold 933.)

A few of the portrait transfers, such as LeBrun and Countess Potocka, and some of the scenic transfers, such as the Mill and Cottage, are found on Steeple marked china as well as on RSP and RSG marked pieces. Unmarked china with such decorations has been put with the Steeple photographs, however, if the mold is a Steeple mold or the background color is unique to Steeple marked pieces.

The Victorian Vignette transfers ("Lady Seated with Dog," "Lady Feeding Chickens," or "Lady Watering Flowers") are also examples of decorations which may be found with one of several of the RS marks. Most often, however, the decoration is on a piece of unmarked china. Because the Steeple mark is found more often with these particular decorations, unmarked examples are included with the Steeple pictures.

To summarize, Steeple marked molds are numbered 1 through 25; Steeple decorations are lettered "A" through "X"; and Steeple Background colors are numbered 1 through 6. Marked Steeple examples are shown first. Unmarked china which matches one of the preceeding Steeple marked molds follows. Steeple Mold 26 (old RSP Mold 51) is shown next. Several RSP molds which are unmarked but which have Steeple decorations follow.

Near the end of this section, I have included pictures of unmarked molds which cannot be matched to Steeple marked molds or other RS marked molds. Because the decoration, however, is one common to Steeple marked china, those pieces have been placed in this section. They have not been assigned any mold numbers. Their status could change if corresponding examples are found with any other mark.

I hope that collectors will study carefully this particular group of photographs of marked and unmarked Steeple china. The Floral Decoration Identification System used here is also used for Ambiguous Marks and Molds.

The very last three photographs shown in the Steeple section are pieces which do have a Steeple mark. The molds or decorations however, are more often found with RSP or RSG marks. Because these items have a Steeple mark, they must be placed in this section. Such pieces simply reflect a transition period between marks and molds.

R.S. Steeple Mark 1 with "Prussia" in red.

R.S. Steeple Mark 2 with "Prussia" in dark green or blue.

R.S. Steeple Mark 3 with "Germany" in red.

R.S. Steeple Mark 4 with "Prussia" in black.

R.S. Steeple Mark 5 with "Germany" in gold.

Plate 44. *Bowl, 10"d, Steeple Mold 2; FDB, multi-colored mums; R.S. Steeple Mark 3.*

Plate 43. *Bowl, 10½"d, Steeple Mold 1; FDA, a pink rose with two yellow roses, a pink bud and two yellow buds; red finish around inner border; gold highlights; R.S. Steeple Mark 5.*

Plate 45. *Cake Plate, 10½"d, Steeple Mold 3; FDC, large white flowers with large green leaves; shadow flowers decorate blue outer border; R.S. Steeple Mark 3.*

Plate 46. *Cake Plate, 11½"d, Steeple Mold 4; FDD, small blue and white wild flowers on long branches; cobalt blue shading to light blue finish with gold highlights; R.S. Steeple Mark 2.*

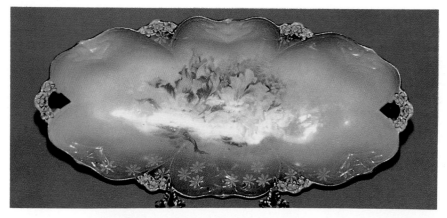

Plate 47. *Celery Tray, 12"l, R.S. Steeple Mold 5; FDE, red and white tulips; green finish on outer border; R.S. Steeple Mark 3.*

Plate 48. *Berry Set: Master Bowl, 9"d; Individual Bowls, 5"d, R.S. Steeple Mold 6 (Iris variation); FDF, on Master Bowl, cluster of small multicolored roses; dark blue shading to light blue finish; R.S. Steeple Mark 3; FDG, large orange poppies with white flowers, on individual bowls.*

Plate 50. *Covered Butter Dish, 5"h; Underplate, 7½"d; R.S. Steeple Mold 6, FDH; border matches Plate in Photograph 49; R.S. Steeple Mark 3.*

Plate 49. *Plate, 9½"d, R.S. Steeple Mold 6; FDH, a large white poppy and a large pink-orange poppy with smaller white flowers; gold stencilled designs on green outer border; R.S. Steeple Mark 3.*

Plate 51. Bowl, R.S. Steeple Mold 7; FDG; light green leaves decorate outer border; shaded brown finish on interior of bowl; gold trim; R.S. Steeple Mark 3.

Plate 52. Tankard, 14¾"h, R.S. Steeple Mold 7; FDI, poppies in shades of lavender (colors vary on this particular transfer); light to dark green finish at top and on lower half of tankard; gold highlights; R.S. Steeple Mark 3.

Plate 53. Dresser Tray, 11½"l x 7¼"w, R.S. Steeple Mold 7; FDJ, cluster of mixed white flowers with green leaves; BG1, wide gold outer border; enameled work on floral designs around outer border; R.S. Steeple Mark 3.

Plate 54. *Bowl, 9"d, R.S. Steeple Mold 7, FDC; BG2, cobalt blue border overlaid with white flowers; gold highlights; R.S. Steeple Mark 3.*

Plate 55. *Cake Plate, 10½"d, R.S. Steeple Mold 7; FDK, bouquet of large flowers in several colors; BG6, Tiffany iridescent finish; gold trim; R.S. Steeple Mark 3.*

Plate 56. *Divided Bowl, 14"l x 9"w, R.S. Steeple Mold 7; FDK; BG6; R.S. Steeple Mark 3.*

Plate 57. Cup, 2"h, and Saucer, R.S. Steeple Mold 7; FDF; BG1; R.S. Steeple Mark 3.

Plate 60. Tankard, 14"h, R.S. Steeple Mold 7; Cottage scenic decor; BG4, pink, green, and orange "glow" background; R.S. Steeple Mark 3.

Plate 58. Cup, 2½"h, and Saucer, R.S. Steeple Mold 7; FDF; BG1; R.S. Steeple Mark 3.

Plate 61. Tankard, 14"h, R.S. Steeple Mold 7; Mill scenic decor; BG4; R.S. Steeple Mark 3.

Plate 59. One handled Dish or Nappy, R.S. Steeple Mold 7; FDL, white flowers with a pink tint, outlined in gold, long slender green leaves; BG3, overall cobalt blue background; R.S. Steeple Mark 3.

29

Plate 62. Bowl, 7¾"d, R.S. Steeple Mold 8; FDC; BG2; gold trim; R.S. Steeple Mark 3.

Plate 63. Celery Tray, 12¼"l x 6"w, R.S. Steeple Mold 8; FDC; BG2; gold trim; R.S. Steeple Mark 3.

Plate 64. Ferner, 2¾"h x 8½"w, R.S. Steeple Mold 8; FD7; gold trim; R.S. Steeple Mark 1.

Plate 65. *Chocolate Pot, R.S. Steeple Mold 8; FDN, cluster of small pink roses; gold enameled stems; BG1, wide gold border with floral decoration repeated over the finish; R.S. Steeple Mark 3.*

Plate 66. *Bowl, 10¾"d, R.S. Steeple Mold 9; FDL, white flowers tinted pink with long green leaves; BG3, cobalt blue overall background; R.S. Steeple Mark 3.*

Plate 67. *Cake Plate, 10¾"d, R.S. Steeple Mold 10; FDL; BG1; R.S. Steeple Mark 3.*

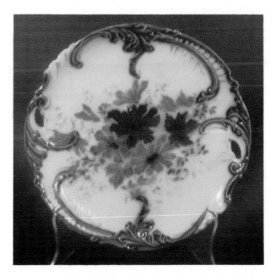

Plate 68. *Cake Plate, 9½"d, R.S. Steeple Mold 11; FDM, floral design painted in blue, shading from light to cobalt; gold trim; R.S. Steeple Mark 3 in dark green.*

Plate 69. *Cake Plate, 9½"d, R.S. Steeple Mold 11; FDO, small white flowers with large leaves, all outlined in gold; BG3; R.S. Steeple Mark 2.*

31

Plate 70. *Chocolate Set: Pot, 10"h; Covered Sugar Bowl and Creamer; R.S. Steeple Mold 12; FDI, purple poppies (colors vary on FDI); R.S. Steeple Mark 3 on Chocolate Pot; Creamer and Sugar are unmarked.*

Plate 71. *Vase, 8¾"h, R.S. Steeple Mold 13; FDQ, a pink, a white, and a yellow mum; shaded light to dark green finish; heavy gold trim; R.S. Steeple Mark 3.*

Plate 72. *Cracker Jar with Creamer and Covered Sugar Bowl; R.S. Steeple Mold 14; FDL on Cracker Jar; FDW, large white flowers outlined in gold, on Creamer and Sugar Bowl; R.S. Steeple Mark 3 on Cracker Jar; Creamer and Sugar are unmarked.*

Plate 73. Plate, 11"d, R.S. Steeple Mold 14; FDC, deep rose colored border shading to light rose; scroll work and pierced part of mold decorated in gold; R.S. Steeple Mark 3.

Plate 74. Chocolate Pot, 10"h, R.S. Steeple Mold 15; FDN, small pink roses; BG1, wide gold border; R.S. Steeple Mark 3.

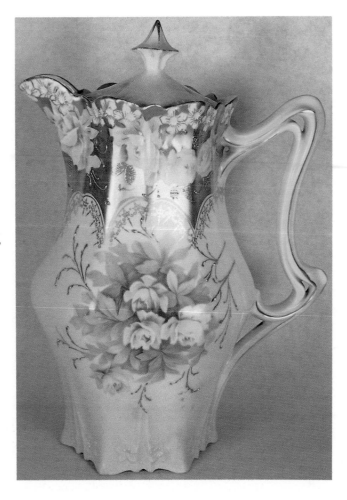

Plate 75. Celery Dish, 11⅛"l x 5½"w, R.S. Steeple Mold 16 (this example is unmarked, but a Steeple marked example of this mold is shown in Plate 543 in G2); FDH, dark green highlights decorated with shadow flowers; white floral shapes of mold outlined in gold.

Plate 76. Bowl, 10¼"d, R.S. Steeple Mold 17; Mill scene; BG4, pink, green, orange "glow" background; gold trim; R.S. Steeple Mark 3.

Plate 77. Plaque, 14"l x 9"w, R.S. Steeple Mold 18; Victorian Vignettes Series: Seated Lady with Dog; R.S. Steeple Mark 3.

Plate 78. *Plaque, 11¼"d, R.S. Steeple Mold 19; Mill scene with BG4; gold highlights border design of mold; R.S. Steeple Mark 3.*

Plate 79. *Plaque, 11¼"d, R.S. Steeple Mold 19; Cottage scene with BG4; R.S. Steeple Mark 3.*

Plate 80. *Vase, R.S. Steeple Mold 20; Queen Louise portrait; cobalt blue finish enhanced with gold designs; R.S. Steeple Mark 1.*

Plate 81. *Reverse side of Vase in Plate 80.*

Plate 82. Vase, 5½"h, R.S. Steeple Mold 21; FDO, BG3; R.S. Steeple Mark 1.

Plate 83. Vase, 7"h, R.S. Steeple Mold 21; FDP, floral design painted in shades of cobalt blue with light gold stems behind design; R.S. Steeple Mark 2.

Plate 84. Celery Tray, 13½"l x 6"w; R.S. Steeple Mold 22; FDP; R.S. Steeple Mark 2.

Plate 85. Syrup Pitcher and Underplate, R.S. Steeple Mold 23; FDP, small flowers decorated in shades of blue from light to cobalt; gold trim; R.S. Steeple Mark 3.

Plate 86. Bowl, 10¼"d, R.S. Steeple Mold 24, Hidden House Mold; FDM, cobalt blue floral design, similar to FDP; R.S. Steeple Mark 2.

Plate 88. *Match Box, 3½"l x 1½"w, FDM; R.S. Steeple Mark 2.*

Plate 87. *Vase, 5½"h, R.S. Steeple Mold 25; FDQ, a pink, a white, and a yellow mum; shaded light to dark green finish; gold trim; R.S. Steeple Mark 3.*

Plate 90. *Inkwell, 4"h, 5½"l; FDM; R.S. Steeple Mark 2.*

Plate 89. *Toothpick Holder, 2¼"h; FDM; gold highlights; R.S. Steeple Mark 2.*

Plate 91. *Card Holder, 4½"w; FDM; R.S. Steeple Mark 2 with "LW" over "50."*

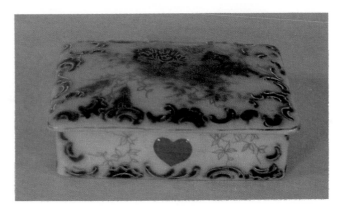

37

Plate 92. *Ashtray or Hatpin Holder (the specific object is difficult to determine), 6"l, small enameled flowers on body with cobalt blue borders, gold trim; R.S. Steeple Mark 3.*

Plate 93. *Covered Box, Egg shaped, 6"l; figural scenic decor of a man in a horse-drawn wagon talking to a woman; R.S. Steeple Mark 5; rare item and rare decoration.*

Plate 94. *Another view of the Egg shaped box in Plate 93.*

Plate 95. *Bowl, 10½"d, R.S. Steeple Mold 1; FDS, yellow roses; gold trim; unmarked.*

Plate 96. *Bowl, 10½"d, R.S. Steeple Mold 1; FDT, spray of multicolored flowers; heavy gold trim on scrolled designs; unmarked.*

Plate 97. *Bowl, R.S. Steeple Mold 2; FDR, a large yellow flower with smaller pink, blue, and white flowers; unmarked.*

Plate 98. *Bowl, 10"d, R.S. Steeple Mold 3; FDF, cluster of small multicolored roses; unmarked.*

Plate 99. Celery Dish, 13¼"l x 6¼"w, R.S. Steeple Mold 3; FDH, green border decorated with white enameled shadow flowers; unmarked.

Plate 100. Bowl, 10½"d, R.S. Steeple Mold 5; FDN, cluster of small pink roses; BG1, heavy gold inner border; unmarked except for an impressed letter "S" on base of bowl. (Whether this initial was meant to indicate "Schlegelmilch," or used for some other purpose is not known.)

Plate 101. Bowl, 10½"d, R.S. Steeple Mold 5; FDG, large orange poppies with white flowers; unmarked.

Plate 102. Relish Dish, 10½"l x 4¾"w, R.S. Steeple Mold 5; FDB, multicolored mums; light pink background with light green tint; gold trim; unmarked.

Plate 103. *Dresser Tray, 11½"l x 7½"w, R.S. Steeple Mold 6; FDH; BG1, heavy gold outer border; gold stencilled inner border; unmarked.*

Plate 105. *Berry Bowl, 5⅝"d, R.S. Steeple Mold 6; FDU, large yellow roses with smaller pink roses; BG1; unmarked.*

Plate 104. *Bowl, 10½"d, R.S. Steeple Mold 6; FDH; BG6, blue and purple iridescent Tiffany finish; unmarked.*

Plate 106. *Relish Dish, 9"l, R.S. Steeple Mold 6; FDA, a pink rose with two yellow roses; BG1; unmarked.*

41

Plate 107. Bowl, 11¼"d, R.S. Steeple Mold 6; FDC; BG6; handpainted small white flowers around inner border; unmarked.

Plate 108. Bowl, 10½"d, R.S. Steeple Mold 6; FDK, bouquet of large flowers in different colors; dark blue inner border with gold stencilled and white enameled flowers; unmarked.

Plate 109. Cracker Jar, 6"h, R.S. Steeple Mold 6; FDG; BG6; unmarked.

Plate 110. Scuttle Shaving Mug, 4"h, R.S. Steeple Mold 6; FDR; pink tint around top border; unmarked.

Plate 111. Scuttle Shaving Mug with Mirror, R.S. Steeple Mold 6; unmarked.

Plate 112. Chocolate Pot, 9¾"h, R.S. Steeple Mold 6; FDF, cluster of small multicolored roses; gold stencilled designs; deep blue top border overlaid with white roses; unmarked.

Plate 113. Chocolate Pot, 9¾"h, R.S. Steeple Mold 6; FDU; deep to light rose tinted top border; gold trim; unmarked.

Plate 114. *Bowl, 10½"d, R.S. Steeple Mold 6; FDK; wide cobalt blue border; gold trim; unmarked.*

Plate 115. *Vase, 9"h, R.S. Steeple Mold 6; FDN, cluster of small pink roses; BG1, wide brilliant gold border; iridescent Tiffany finish on lower body; gold handles; unmarked.*

Plate 116. *Bowl, 8¾"d, R.S. Steeple Mold 7; FDS, large yellow roses; BG1; FDN around inner border; unmarked.*

Plate 117. Chocolate Pot, 12"h, R.S. Steeple Mold 7; FDA; unmarked.

Plate 118. Chocolate Pot with Cup and Saucer, R.S. Steeple Mold 7; FDV, 2 large pink roses with a watered silk finish; unmarked.

Plate 119. *Cake Plate, 11"d, R.S. Steeple Mold 8; FDI, poppies with a lavender to orange to yellow tint; green background; gold trim; unmarked.*

Plate 120. *Cake Plate, 11"d, R.S. Steeple Mold 8; FDC; BG2, white flowers on cobalt blue border; unmarked.*

Plate 122. *Bowl, 10"d, R.S. Steeple Mold 8; Lady Watering Flowers from Victorian Vignettes series; BG5, green border overlaid with white flowers; unmarked.*

Plate 121. *Bowl, 9"d, R.S. Steeple Mold 8; Diana the Huntress center decor with cupids in reserves around inner border; BG6, iridescent Tiffany border finish; gold trim; unmarked.*

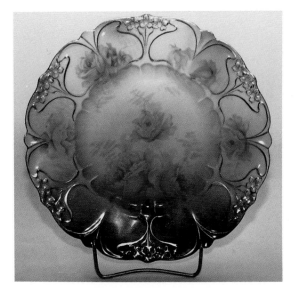

Plate 124. Plate, 8½"d, R.S. Steeple Mold 10; FDV, large pink roses with watered silk finish; gold stencilled designs; unmarked.

Plate 123. Bowl, 10¾"d, R.S. Steeple Mold 9; FDU, yellow and pink roses; rose finish around inner border; unmarked.

Plate 125. Plate, 10¾"d, R.S. Steeple Mold 10; FDN; BG1; unmarked.

Plate 126. Covered Sugar Bowl, 5"h, and Creamer, 3½"h; R.S. Steeple Mold 12; FDE on Sugar Bowl and FDH on Creamer; deep to light rose tinted finish; gold borders; unmarked.

Plate 127. Teapot, 6"h, R.S. Steeple Mold 12; FDU, yellow and pink roses; rose tinted finish and gold border; unmarked.

Plate 128. Tea Set: Teapot, 5½"h; Covered Sugar Bowl, 5"h; Creamer, 4"h; R.S. Steeple Mold 12; FDI, lavender and orange tinted poppies on green background; unmarked.

Plate 129. *Vase, 8¾"h, R.S. Steeple Mold 12; Countess Potocka portrait; pearlized green finish on body with BG6, iridescent Tiffany borders; unmarked.*

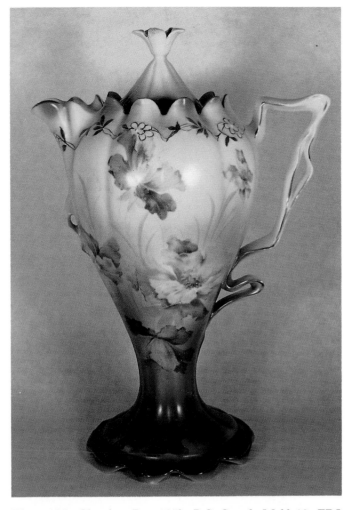

Plate 130. *Chocolate Pot, 10"h, R.S. Steeple Mold 12; FDI, purple and orange poppies; shaded light to dark green background; matte finish; unmarked.*

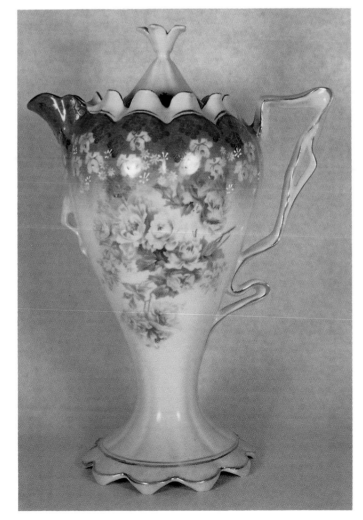

Plate 131. *Chocolate Pot, 10"h, R.S. Steeple Mold 12; FDF; rose tinted finish; unmarked.*

Plate 132. *Chocolate Set: Pot, 10"h; Cups, 3"h; R.S. Steeple Mold 14; FDE; unmarked.*

Plate 133. *Demi-tasse Cup, 2¾"h, and Saucer, R.S. Steeple Mold 14; FDE, tulips; background shades from cream to brown; unmarked.*

Plate 134. *Tea Set: Covered Sugar Bowl, 3¼"h; Teapot, 6½"h; and Creamer, 3¼"h; R.S. Steeple Mold 14; FDW; BG3; unmarked.*

Plate 135. *Cracker Jar, 7½"h, R.S. Steeple Mold 14; FDW, large white flower outlined in gold; BG3, overall cobalt blue finish on body; unmarked.*

Plate 136. *Vase, 7"h, R.S. Steeple Mold 14; FDU, yellow and pink roses; BG3; unmarked.*

Plate 137. Covered Sugar Bowl, 4½"h, and Teapot, 6"h; R.S. Steeple Mold 15; FDN, cluster of small pink roses; BG1, wide brilliant gold border; unmarked.

Plate 138. Cracker Jar, 5½"h x 9"w, R.S. Steeple Mold 16; FDR, large yellow flower with smaller blue, white, and pink flowers; semi-gloss finish; unmarked.

Plate 139. Plate, 9"d, R.S. Steeple Mold 26; FDX, large white water lilies outlined in gold with enameled gold leaves; BG3, cobalt blue body finish; unmarked.

51

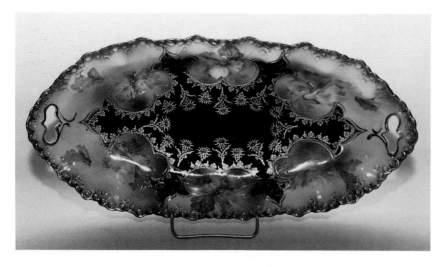

Plate 140. Celery Dish, 13½"l x 6½"w, R.S. Steeple Mold 26; FDI decorates border; dark green finish covers center of dish overlaid with gold stencilled flowers; unmarked.

Plate 141. Tea Set: Covered Sugar Bowl, Teapot, and Creamer; R.S. Steeple Mold 26; FDU, yellow and pink roses on Sugar Bowl; FDE, tulips on Teapot; and FDH, white and pink-orange poppies on Creamer; unmarked.

Plate 142. Shaving Mug, 3½"h, R.S. Steeple Mold 26; FDH; unmarked.

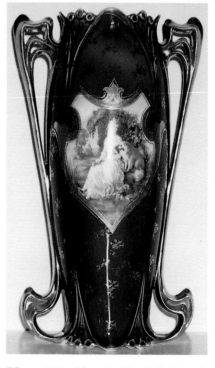

Plate 143. Vase, 14"h, R.S. Steeple Mold 26; Lady seated with Dog figural portrait decor; BG3, cobalt blue finish; small gold floral designs; gold framework outlining portrait; gold trim; unmarked.

Plate 144. Dresser Tray, RSP Mold 23; FDS, large yellow roses; unmarked.

Plate 145. Chocolate Pot, 11"h, RSP Mold 525 (companion to RSP Mold 23); FDA, pink and yellow roses; cobalt blue finish at top and on base; unmarked.

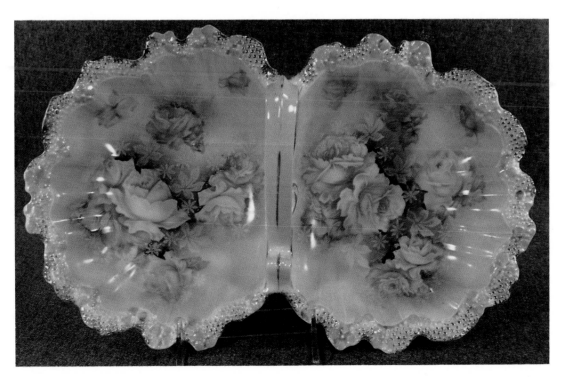

Plate 146. Divided Bowl with handle, 14½"l, RSP Mold 23; FDS, yellow roses with FDV, two large pink roses (without watered silk finish); unmarked.

Plate 147. *Chocolate Set: Pot, 9¾"h, and Cups and Saucers; RSP Mold 525; FDS and FDV; unmarked.*

Plate 148. *Chocolate Set: Pot, 9¾"h, and Cups and Saucers; RSP Mold 525; FDA; red finish on inner border under stippled top borders; gold trim; unmarked.*

Plate 149. *Berry Bowl, 5¾"d, RSP Mold 29; FDS; gold stencilled designs; unmarked.*

Plate 150. *Cake Plate, 9¾"d, RSP Mold 29; FDT, spray of multicolored flowers; shades of green highlight inner borders; unmarked.*

Plate 151. *Bowl, 10½"d, RSP Mold 29; FDS, large yellow roses; blue outer border decorated with a gold Greek key design; luster finish; unmarked.*

Plate 152. *Bowl, 10⅜"d, variation of RSP Mold 29; FDV, 2 large pink roses, without watered silk finish, center decorated with FDN, small pink roses, around inner border; BG1, wide brilliant gold border; unmarked.*

Plate 153. *Tea Set: Covered Sugar Bowl, 4¾"h; Teapot, 5¼"h; Creamer, 3¾"h; RSP Mold 517 (companion to RSP Mold 29); FDN, cluster of small pink roses; gold enameled leaves; glossy finish; unmarked.*

Plate 154. *Chocolate Pot, 9½"h, RSP Mold 517; FDN; gold enameled leaves; unmarked.*

Plate 155. *Demi-tasse Cup, 2¼"h, and Saucer, RSP Mold 517; FDN; BG1; unmarked.*

Plate 156. *Coffee Pot, 9½"h, RSP Mold 517; FDA, pink and white roses; blue-green border decorated with white shadow flowers; unmarked.*

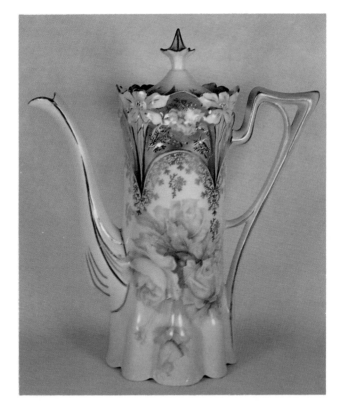

Plate 157. *Coffee Pot, 9½"h, RSP Mold 517; FDS, large yellow roses; BG1, wide brilliant gold border; unmarked.*

Plate 158. *Bowl, 10"d, RSP Mold 87; FDR, large yellow flower with blue, white, and pink smaller flowers; unmarked.*

Plate 159. *Bowl, RSP Mold 98; FDS, large yellow roses; dark green border overlaid with gold Greek Key design; unmarked.*

Plate 160. *Relish Dish, 9½"l x 4½"w, RSP Mold 98; FDN, cluster of small pink roses; gold trim; unmarked.*

Plate 161. *Cake Plate, 10"d, RSP Mold 98; FDT, spray of multicolored flowers; large single pink or yellow roses on blue-green background decorate border; unmarked.*

Plate 162. *Berry Set, RSP Mold 98; Cottage scene decorates master Bowl and three of the individual bowls (only one shown); Castle scene decorates the other three bowls (only one shown); BG4, pink, green, and orange "glow" background; unmarked.*

Plate 163. *Oval two handled Bowl, 13"l x 8"w, RSP Mold 98; Lady seated with Dog figural decor; unmarked.*

Plate 164. *Celery Dish, 12¼"l x 6"w, RSP Mold 339; FDA, pink and white roses in center of dish with FDW around border; unmarked.*

Plate 165. *Cake Plate, 11"d, RSP Mold 339; FDA; BG1; unmarked.*

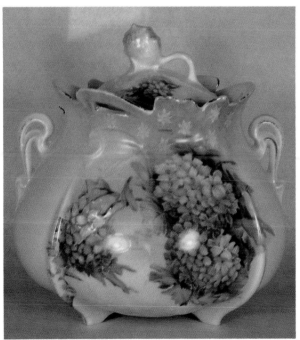

Plate 167. *Cracker Jar, 7"h x 6"w, RSP Mold 657; green and white snowballs; semi-gloss finish; unmarked.*

Plate 166. *Divided Dish (or Cabaret) with center handle, 14"l, RSP Mold 347; FDD, small blue and white wild flowers; tinted blue background; unmarked.*

Plate 168. Tea Set: Covered Sugar Bowl, 4"h; Teapot, 5½"h; Creamer, 4"h; RSP Mold 664; FDT, spray of multicolored flowers; tinted green background; unmarked.

Plate 169. Tea Set: Creamer, Teapot, Covered Sugar Bowl; RSP Mold 664; Cottage and Castle scenes; BG4, pink, green, and orange "glow" background; unmarked.

Plate 170. Toothpick Holder, 2¾"h, RSP Mold 664; FDA; gold stencilled designs; lavender highlights; unmarked.

Plate **171.** *Chocolate Pot, 9¼"h, RSP Mold 664; FDT decorates body; top border has single pink and yellow roses on blue-green background; unmarked.*

Plate **172.** *Demi-tasse Pot, 9"h, RSP Mold 664; FDS, tinted green background; unmarked.*

Plate 173. Bowl, *a floral border mold; FDS, large yellow roses; cobalt blue border highlighted with gold; unmarked.*

Plate 174. Bowl, 10¾"d (a pleated mold); FDS, large yellow roses; unmarked.

Plate 175. Bowl, 10¼"d, a floral border mold; FDC, large white flowers with large green leaves; green outer edge highlighted with gold; unmarked.

Plate 176. Bowl, 10½"d, a "dome" shaped mold; FDK, bouquet of large flowers in several colors; unmarked.

Plate 177. Bowl, unusual body shape mold; FDT, spray of multicolored flowers; black finish on three "dome" sections overlaid with gold floral designs; unmarked.

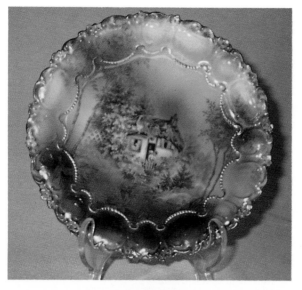

Plate 178. Wall Plaque, 7½"d, floral border mold; Cottage scene; BG4, pink to green to orange "glow" background; unmarked.

Plate 179. Bowl, 9¾"d, a "dome" shaped mold; Lady Feeding Chickens figural decor; Tiffany bronze finish; unmarked.

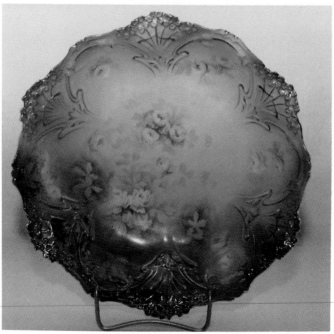

Plate 180. Bowl, 10"d, a "dome" mold with a floral border; FDN, cluster of small pink roses; cream to shaded blue-green background; unmarked. (The following three photographs are examples of this mold.)

Plate 181. *Bowl, 11½"d, a square version of the mold in Plate 180; FDC, large white flowers with large green leaves; unmarked.*

Plate 182. *Bowl, 10½"d; FDE, tulips; tinted blue background; unmarked.*

Plate 183. *Ice Cream Bowl or Tray, 11½"l x 9"w; FDG, large orange poppies with white flowers; tinted green background; unmarked.*

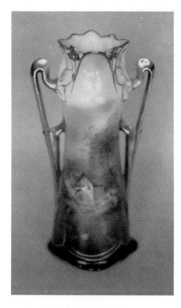

Plate 184. *Vase, 7"h; Mill scene; BG4, pink to green to orange "glow" background; gold trim; unmarked.*

Plate 185. *Plaque, 13"l x 9¼"w (this mold is similar to the one shown in Plate 77); Lady Seated with Fan; yellow to green tinted background; unmarked.*

Plate 186. *Chocolate Pot, 9½"h, footed; FDI, purple to yellow to orange tinted poppies; light yellow to dark green background; unmarked.*

Plate 187. *Cracker Jar, 5"h x 6¾"d, an RSG style mold; blue butterfly decor; gold trim; R.S. Steeple Mark 5.*

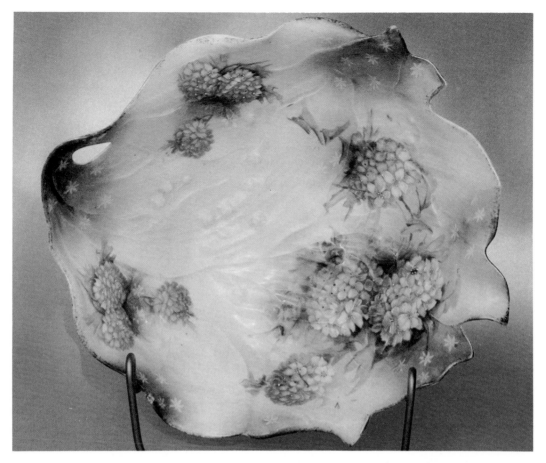

Plate 188. *Leaf Bowl, 9"l x 8"w, RSP Mold 10; snowballs on tinted green background; R.S. Steeple Mark 5.*

Plate 189. *Plate, 8"d, RSP Mold 93; RSP FD2, multicolored roses; rose finish on dome sections; gold trim; R.S. Steeple Mark 3.*

R.S. Germany

The R.S. Germany wreath mark is probably the least controversial of all RS marks. The mark apparently was used only at the Tillowitz factory. From catalog advertisements, the mark is noted to have been in use a few years prior to World War I. It probably overlapped the R.S. Tillowitz and R.S. Silesia marks used during the 1930s and 1940s. Two styles of script marks were also used. Those marks and their variations are shown here. The double marks illustrate the transition of one mark to another.

RSG Mark 1 shows the Steeple mark with the gold script "hand-painted" RSG mark. Mark 2 is the gold script mark without any additional mark. Mark 3 includes the RSP mark with the gold script mark. Marks 4 and 5 illustrate a different form of script mark. This mark is fancier than the gold one. It is a transfer rather than a stamped mark and appears to be later than the gold script mark. Mark 6 shows the underglaze RSG wreath mark together with the overglaze RSP mark. Marks 3 through 6 clearly indicate that the RSP mark was on china exported from the Tillowitz factory. It is still unclear whether the RSP mark was used at the Tillowitz factory shortly after that factory opened or whether it was only used for a few years while the Suhl factory was in transition to the Tillowitz location, circa 1917.

Marks 7 through 12 are examples of the RSG wreath marks with slight variations in different colors. Marks 13 and 14 show the RSG mark with an additional mark for American importers.

The RSG marks are found on china which usually contrasts sharply with china bearing some of the other RS marks. The molds are simple, and the decoration is predominantly floral, fashioned in a very artistic, stylized design. This type of decoration as well as the simple shapes were popular during the 1920s. When the RSG mark is found on an RSP or Steeple mold, the mark merely indicates that an old mold continued to be used and was marked with the later RSG mark.

The photographs are divided into Flat and Vertical Objects. A few RSP molds are shown in the first pictures of the Flat Objects. The other examples in that category are grouped according to the type of floral decoration. The Vertical Objects are presented by type of object in an alphabetical order. Some unmarked pieces have been included under the RSG marks because of their simple molds and stylized decoration.

R.S. Germany Mark 1, R.S. Steeple Mark with "hand-painted, R.S. Germany" script mark in gold.

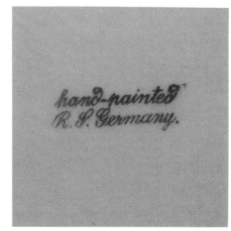

R.S. Germany Mark 2, R.S. Germany script mark in gold with "hand-painted."

R.S. Germany Mark 3, R.S. Prussia red wreath mark with "hand-painted R.S. Germany" script mark in gold.

R.S. Germany Mark 4, R.S. Prussia green wreath mark with "Reinhold Schlegelmilch, Tillowitz, Germany" red script mark.

R.S. Germany Mark 5, R.S. Prussia red wreath mark with "Reinhold Schlegelmilch, Tillowitz, Germany" red script mark.

R.S. Germany Mark 6, R.S. Prussia red wreath mark with blue R.S. Germany wreath mark (underglaze).

R.S. Germany Mark 7, R.S. Germany blue wreath mark with red "Reinhold Schlegelmilch, Tillowitz, Germany" script mark.

R.S. Germany Mark 8, R.S. Germany blue wreath mark.

R.S. Germany Mark 9, green wreath mark.

R.S. Germany Mark 10, R.S. Germany green wreath mark with slight variation from Mark 9.

R.S. Germany Mark 11, R.S. Germany green wreath mark with "Handpainted."

R.S. Germany Mark 12, gold wreath mark.

R.S. Germany Mark 13, green wreath mark with "BT CO." mark (American importing firm, probably Burley-Tyrrell in Chicago).

R.S. Germany Mark 14, blue wreath mark with "MW" (Montgomery Ward, American importer); "Handpainted" and "warranted 18 carat gold" additional markings.

Plate 190. *Oval Bowl, two handles, 8½" x 13", RSP Mold 25 (Iris Mold); Summer Season portrait; white satin finish; RSG Mark 9.*

Plate 191. *Cake Plate, 11"d, RSP Mold 25a (Iris variation Mold); Steeple Floral Decoration "F," cluster of multicolored roses; RSG Mark 9.*

Plate 192. *Cake Plate, 10½"d, RSP Mold 28 (Carnation Mold); bronze and orange mums; unmarked (decoration is an RSG transfer, see Plate 351).*

Plate 203. *Cake Plate; RSG Cottage scene II (a large white house with two smaller houses in the background); shaded green background gives a wooded effect; RSG Mark 10.*

Plate 204. *Bowl, 10½"d; RSG Cottage scene II; brown tone finish on wooded scenery; RSG Mark 10.*

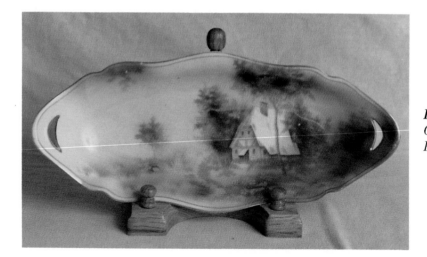

Plate 205. *Celery Tray, 12¾"l x 5¾"w; RSG Cottage scene I (white house with a thatched roof); RSG Mark 10.*

Plate 206. *Bowl, pierced handles, footed, 6" x 8"; Relish Dish, 10½" x 5⅛"; RSG Mill scene (not the same as the Mill scene found on RSP marked china). There are two views of this scene with one featured on each dish; RSG Mark 8.*

74

Plate 207. *Plate, 8½"d; figural portrait of a white robed woman holding a bouquet of white flowers; white lilies with gold stems on red background decorate panels on either side of portrait; gold trim; RSG Mark 9.*

Plate 208. *Plate, 8"d; white apple blossoms; "Lenbach" signature, decoration appears to be factory rather than amateur; RSG Mark 11.*

Plate 209. *One handled Dish or Nappy, 7⅛"l; Cotton Plant pattern; RSG Mark 8 with "Cottonplant handpainted, MWCo."*

Plate 210. Bowl, 10¼" x 9", pierced handles; pink carnations; shaded green background; RSG Mark 9.

Plate 211. Relish Dish, 10¼" x 4½"; stylized white chrysanthemums; unmarked except for "Handpainted" gold script mark (as in Mark 10).

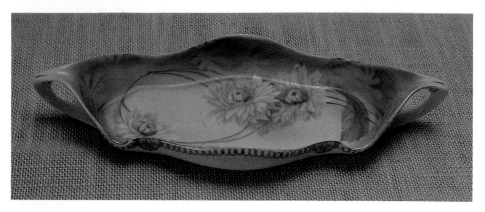

Plate 212. Plate; yellow daffodil; dark to light green background; RSG Mark 8.

Plate 213. Plate, 9¾"d; large white daisies; RSG Mark 8.

Plate 215. *Footed Bowl, 6¼"d; RSP FD97, Dogwood and Pine on tinted brown background, RSG Mark 8.*

Plate 214. *Cake Plate, 10"d; RSP FD97, Dogwood and Pine decor with dark green border; RSG Mark 8.*

Plate 216. *Plate, 8½"d; pink tinted iris with gold leaves; RSG Mark 7.*

Plate 217. *Plate, 6½"d; white and pink iris; gold trim; RSG Mark 7.*

Plate 218. *Cake Plate, 10"d; pink orchids on shaded brown background; RSG Mark 9.*

Plate 219. *Cake Plate, 10"d; pink orchids on tinted green background; gold trim; RSG Mark 8.*

Plate 221. *Sandwich Plate, 4"h, 10½"d; dark and light pink lilies; unmarked, floral decor is an RSG transfer.*

Plate 220. *Plate, 8½"d; clusters of tiny white flowers with a lilac tint; shaded green background; RSG Mark 8.*

Plate 222. Celery Set: Tray, 10½" x 5"; Salt Dips, 2¾" x 2"; white lilies; gold trim; RSG Mark 9.

Plate 223. Plate, 8¼"d; white lilies; blue inner border with gold stencilled designs; RSG Mark 9.

Plate 224. *Relish Dish, pierced work on sides; white lilies; fancy gold stencilled designs around outer border; RSG Mark 9.*

Plate 225. *Relish Dish, molded handles; pink and white lilies; gold egg and dart design around border; satin finish; RSG Mark 9.*

Plate 226. Plate, 6⅜"d; Lily of the Valley with large gold leaves; RSG Mark 7.

Plate 227. Tray, 8" x 4⅛"; unusual sided mold with pierced work on sides; pink, orange, and white peonies; unmarked.

Plate 228. Plate, 8⅜"d; stylized white peonies on shaded green background; RSG Mark 11.

Plate 229. *Plate, 8¼"d; pink tinted poppies; gold trim; RSG Mark 11.*

Plate 230. *Dresser Tray, 12"l x 7¼"w; white poppies with a green tint; pearl luster finish; RSG Mark 9.*

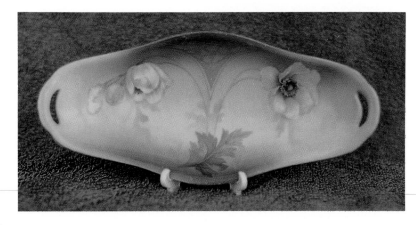

Plate 231. *Relish Dish, 8"l; stylized white poppies; RSG Mark 11 without "Handpainted."*

Plate 232. *Berry Set; orange poppies; RSG Mark 9.*

Plate 233. *Relish Dish, 9½"l x 4¼"w; orange poppies; RSG Mark 9.*

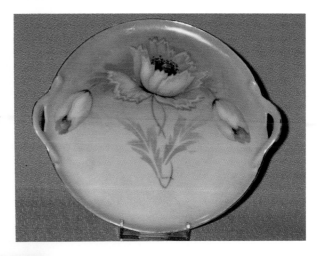

Plate 234. *Tray or Chop Plate, pierced handles, 7¼"d; yellow poppies on shaded orange background; luster finish; RSG Mark 9.*

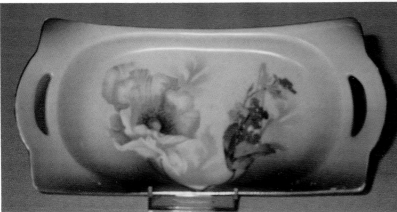

Plate 235. *Relish Dish, pierced handles, 8½"l x 4"w; orange poppy with small blue flowers; RSG Mark 10.*

Plate 236. *Plate, 8"d; pink roses; RSG Mark 8.*

Plate 237. *Footed Bowl, 3 knob feet, 2⅜"h, 7½"d; light pink and dark pink roses; RSG Mark 8.*

Plate 238. *Two Handled Dish, 6⅞" x 8½"; pink roses; unmarked.*

Plate 239. Berry Set; stylized white roses with an orange tint; Art Nouveau scroll work; RSG Mark 11 without "Handpainted."

Plate 240. Two Handled Dish; stylized pink and orange roses; RSG Mark 9.

Plate 241. Plate, 6½"d; peach roses; gold stencilled design around border; satin finish; RSG Mark 8 with "Royal Vienna" in gold.

Plate 242. Two Handled Dish with a semi-rolled edge, 9"l x 4½"w; pink and white roses; RSG Mark 11.

Plate 243. *Cake Set; stylized pink roses with small light orange roses on top border with a dark orange background; RSG Mark 8.*

Plate 244. *Cake Plate, 9¾"d; white roses with a yellow tint; RSG Mark 9.*

Plate 245. *Two Handled Dish, flat base, 10"d; white roses; beige border decorated with small white flowers outlined in gold; gold stencilled design on inner border; RSG Mark 11.*

Plate 246. *Charger, 12½"d; large white roses with a yellow tint; gold tapestry design at top of plate; RSG Mark 7.*

Plate 247. Bowl, 10"d; single white roses around inner border and in center; fancy leaf designs on brown background decorate center; RSG Mark 9.

Plate 248. Celery Dish, 14"l x 6½"w; yellow tinted roses; RSG Mark 9.

Plate 249. Bowl, 9½" x 8", unusual mold with 3 square sides and rounded at the top; white roses; RSG Mark 9.

Plate 250. Plate, 8½"d; white roses; gold stencilled work at top of plate and around inner border; RSG Mark 7.

Plate 251. One Handled Dish or Nappy; orange and yellow roses; pearl luster finish; RSG Mark 8.

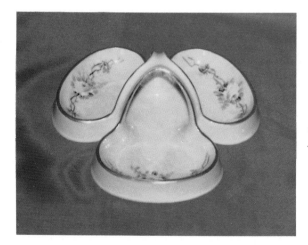

Plate 252. Clover shaped Dish with 3 part handle; small pink roses; gold trim; RSG Mark 8 with artist signature "Marie Edelman," non-factory decoration.

Plate 253. Relish Dish, 8"l x 3¾"w; pink roses with snowballs and light yellow roses with snowballs decorate inner border; gold trim; RSG Mark 8 with "Hand-painted" in gold and "Germany" impressed.

Plate 254. *Plate, 8½"d; pale pink and yellow rose clusters around inner border; brown outer border; gold scroll work; RSG Mark 8.*

Plate 255. *Berry Bowl, 5½"d; roses and rose garlands around inner border; gold trim; RSG Mark 6.*

Plate 256. *Bowl, 10"d; white wild roses; RSG Mark 8.*

Plate 257. *One Handled Dish or Nappy, 7¾"l x 5"w; rust and tan wild roses; gold trim; RSG Mark 9.*

Plate 258. Footed Bowl, 8¼"l x 6"w; pink and white wild roses; gold tapestry design at top of bowl; RSG Mark 8.

Plate 259. One Handled Dish or Nappy, 7½"l x 4¾"w; wild roses with a pink tint; RSG Mark 14.

Plate 260. Cake Plate, 10"d; white and pink wild roses; gold tapestry design on gray background; RSG Mark 8.

Plate 261. Cake Plate, 11"d; rust and white wild roses; gold trim; RSG Mark 7.

Plate 262. Cake Plate, 11"d; pink peonies and snowballs; gold trim; RSG Mark 9 without "Germany."

Plate 263. Cake Set: Cake Plate, 10¾"d; Individual Plates, 6¾"d; pink peonies and snowballs; unmarked.

Plate 264. Bowl, 5¼"d, and Ladle (sauce or mayonnaise dish); snowballs; gold stencilled designs around inner border; gold trim; RSG Mark 9.

Plate 265. *Two Handled Dish in an unusual shape, 8½"l x 6"w; pink and white tulips; gold stencilled designs; gold trim; RSG Mark 8.*

Plate 266. *Bowl, 9¾"d; pink and yellow tulips; gold finish at top of bowl; RSG Mark 8.*

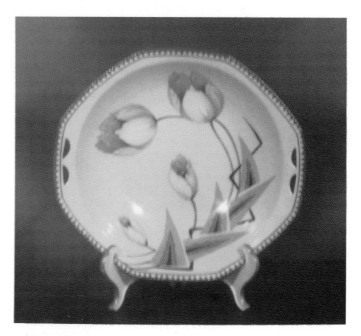

Plate 267. *Bowl, 9"d; orange tulips; double pierced handles; RSG Mark 9.*

Plate 268. *Bowl with rolled edge; large pink and white floral buds; gold trim; RSG Mark 9.*

Plate 269. *Cake Plate, 10½"d; Steeple Floral Decoration "K" with red poinsettias; RSG Mark 10.*

Plate 270. *Cake Plate, 11"d, ornately scrolled mold; small lilac colored flowers on tinted green background; RSG Mark 8.*

Plate 271. *Relish Dish, 8⅝"l x 4⅜"w; large lavender flowers with green to brown shaded leaves on a black background; RSG Mark 8.*

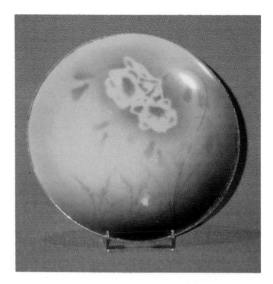

Plate 272. *Plate, 6"d; white shadow flower decor on a gray background; RSG Mark 11 without "Handpainted."*

Plate 273. *Bowl, 5½"l x 4"w, triangular shaped mold with pierced work on one end; light and dark blue geometric designs in an Art Deco style; wide gold outer border; RSG Mark 8.*

Plate 274. *Bowl, 6½"l x 5½"w; molded Indian profile at top of bowl; gold finish decorated with engraved designs; RSG Mark 8.*

Plate 275. *Tray, 8½"l x 4¼"w; gold stencilled floral and leaf designs; gold handles; RSG Mark 12.*

Plate 276. *Cake Set; lavender and white pearl luster finish; clusters of straw flowers decorate center and outer border; RSG Mark 8.*

Plate 277. *Two Handled Dish, 8"l; molded birds in center of handles; pearl luster finish; small hand-painted flowers; gold trim; RSG wreath mark, uncolored, similar to the uncolored R.S. Silesia Mark (see R.S. Silesia Mark 9).*

Plate 278. *Bowl, 6½" x 5½"; yellow and green marbled pearl luster finish; RSG Mark 8.*

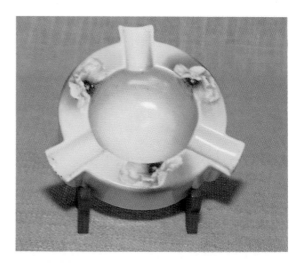

Plate 280. Ashtray, 3¾"d; orange poppies; RSG Mark 10.

Plate 279. Bowl, 7"d; clover shape; marbled blue and orange pearl luster finish; RSG Mark 8.

Plate 281. Basket; pearl luster finish, handpainted flowers, gold trim; RSG uncolored wreath mark as in Plate 277.

Plate 282. Basket, 4"h; hand-painted small pink roses; gold trim; RSG Mark 8; non-factory decoration.

Plate 283. *Covered Box, 4½" x 3"; leaf shape, RSP Mold 834; RSP FD25, Magnolias; RSG Mark 10 with a raised 6 point star. (See Ambiguous Marks for other examples of this mold.)*

Plate 284. *Covered Box, 3½" x 4", heart shaped mold. This box and the boxes in Plates 285 and 286 are shaped for suits of playing cards. Each box has an embossed heart, spade, or club on the bottom and an embossed shamrock on the top; pink peony and snowball decor; RSG Mark 10.*

Plate 286. *Covered Box, club shaped; white lily; RSG Mark 10.*

Plate 285. *Covered Box, 3½" x 4", spade shaped; white flowers; RSG Mark 10.*

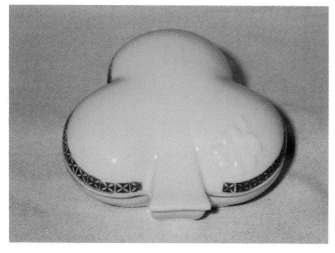

Plate 287. *Covered Box, club shaped; gold trim; RSG Mark 11 without "Handpainted."*

Plate 288. *Covered Box, 3¼"h, 3"d; RSP FD79, Calla Lily; RSG Mark 8.*

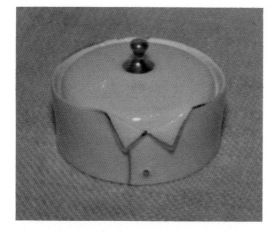

Plate 289. *Covered Box for studs or collar buttons, 2¾"d; note shirt collar points; gold trim; RSG Mark 8.*

Plate 290. *Covered Box, 4½"d; pale yellow roses with brown highlights; RSG Mark 10.*

Plate 291. *Covered Box, 4½"d; orange poppies; RSG Mark 10.*

Plate 292. *Coffee Pot, 9"h; white flowers with green leaves; tinted green to brown finish; RSG Mark 9.*

Plate 293. *Chocolate Set: Pot, 9½"h, and Cups and Saucers; white lilies with pink highlights; gold stencilled designs; gold trim; RSG Mark 9.*

Plate 294. *Chocolate Pot, individual size, 7¼"h; large white poppies on tan tinted background; glossy finish; RSG Mark 9.*

Plate 295. *Pieces from a Dinner Service: Coffee Pot, Sugar Bowl, Creamer, Cups and Saucers, Salt Shaker, Cake Plate, Mustard Pot, Jam Jar, small Plates; pattern composed of small pink roses with green leaves; gold trim; RSG Mark 8 in blue.*

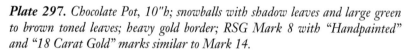

Plate 296. Chocolate Set: Pot, 9½"h; Cups, 3"h, and Saucers; large white petaled flowers on tinted brown background; RSG Mark 7.

Plate 297. Chocolate Pot, 10"h; snowballs with shadow leaves and large green to brown toned leaves; heavy gold border; RSG Mark 8 with "Handpainted" and "18 Carat Gold" marks similar to Mark 14.

Plate 298. Chocolate Set: Pot and Cups and Saucers; large roses on shaded brown background; gold trim; RSG Mark 7.

Plate 299. Chocolate Set: Pot, 10"h, and Cups and Saucers; white apple blossoms; green leaves; glossy finish; RSG Mark 8.

Plate 300. Chocolate Set: Pot, 10"h; Cups, 3"h, and Saucers; Art Deco Mold; RSG Cottage scene II with green trees and grass; each piece has a different view of the cottages; RSG Mark 10.

Plate 301. Chocolate Set: Pot, 9"h; Cups, 2⅞"h, and Saucers; stylized roses; RSG Mark 10 on Pot; RSG Mark 13 on Cups; only "BT" part of Mark 13 on Saucers.

Plate 302. Cider Pitcher, 5"h x 10"w; yellow and white tulips; high glaze finish; RSG Mark 8.

Plate 304. *Creamer, 3½"h; Swans with Evergreens decor; unmarked (RSG Mold).*

Plate 303. *Creamer, 4½"h; yellow daffodils; pearl luster finish; RSG Mark 8.*

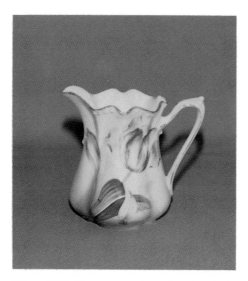

Plate 306. *Creamer, 3¼"h; stylized pink roses; satin finish; RSG Mark 10.*

Plate 305. *Creamer, 4"h; pink tulips; RSG Mark 8.*

Plate 307. *Creamer, 3¼"h; and Covered Sugar Bowl, 4¼"h; pink poppies; gold trim; RSG Mark 8.*

Plate 308. *Covered Sugar Bowl, 5⅜"h; and Creamer, 4⅛"h; light orange poppies on darker orange background; high gloss finish; variation of green wreath RSG Mark 9.*

Plate 309. *Covered Sugar Bowl, 3¼"h; and Creamer, 3½"h; RSP Mold 534; pink roses; gold trim; RSG Mark 10.*

Plate 310. *Creamer, 2¾"h; and Covered Sugar, 5"h; Lettuce Mold; pearl luster finish; RSG Mark 9.*

Plate 311. Covered Sugar Bowl, 3¾"h; and Creamer, 2½"h; white roses; gold trim; RSG Mark 9.

Plate 312. Creamer, 2⅜"h; and Covered Sugar Bowl, 4"h; pink tinted iris; RSG Mark 8.

Plate 313. Covered Sugar Bowl, 3¾"h; white flowers; RSG Mark 9.

Plate 314. *Covered Sugar Bowl, 3¾"h; RSP FD18, a large open white poppy and a closed orange poppy; wide gold border; RSG Mark 9.*

Plate 315. *Covered Sugar Bowl, 3"h; pink and white roses; RSG Mark 8.*

Plate 316. *Covered Sugar Bowl, 4"d; orange poppies; RSG Mark 9.*

Plate 317. *Covered Sugar Bowl; light and dark pink roses; RSG Mark 10.*

Plate 318. *Covered Sugar Bowl; RSP FD92, cluster of small purple and white flowers with pale peach roses; RSG Mark 10.*

Plate 319. *Covered Sugar Bowl, 4⅝"h; white roses on green to brown tinted background; RSG Mark 9.*

105

Plate 321. Demi-tasse Cup; RSP FD79, Calla Lily; RSG Mark 8.

Plate 320. Cup and Saucer; RSP Mold 517 (Lily Mold); RSP FD7, pink and white roses; dark green finish on borders; RSG Mark 2 on cup; saucer is unmarked.

Plate 322. Cup, 2¼"h, and Saucer; pink and white flowers; gold stencilled border design; white to beige background; pearl luster finish; RSG Mark 8.

Plate 323. Cup, 3½"h, and Saucer; RSP Mold 462; yellow daffodil; heavy gold trim; RSG Mark 9.

Plate 324. Demi-tasse Cup, 1½"h and Saucer; white lilies with pink tint on pale green to beige background; RSG wreath mark in red, rare mark.

Plate 325. Cup, 1¾"h, and Saucer; red-orange and white flowers; gold trim; RSG Mark 7 on saucer and RSG Mark 8 on cup.

Plate 326. Cup, 3¼"h, and Saucers; RSP FD89, pink and white tulips; large gold leaves; RSG Mark 8 on the cups and red script mark from RSG Mark 7 on the saucers.

Plate 327. Cup, 2"h, and Saucer; white apple blossoms on shaded white to brown background; RSG Mark 8.

Plate 328. Demi-tasse Cup, 3"h, and Saucer; small white flowers; wide gold border; RSG Mark 8.

Plate 329. Cracker Jar, 5½"h x 9"w, RSP Mold 517 (Lily Mold); pink and white roses on shaded green background; RSG Mark 2.

Plate 330. Cracker Jar, 5½"h x 8½"w; pink and white wild roses; gold tapestry design on gray background around top of jar; gold trim; RSG Mark 8.

Plate 331. Cracker Jar, 5½"h, light cream colored carnations with a pink tint; RSG Mark 8.

Plate 334. Ferner or Flower Holder with Frog; white roses; gold trim; RSG Mark 8 with "Handpainted."

Plate 332. Ewer, 5½"h, RSP Mold 640; white lilies; RSG Mark 11 without "Handpainted."

Plate 333. Ewer, 5½"h, RSP Mold 640; white poppies; RSG Mark 10.

Plate 335. *Hair Receiver, 2½"h; large white flowers on base with an orange tinted bud on lid; pierced handles on each side; RSG Mark 8.*

Plate 336. *Hatpin Holders, 4½"h: left, double white poppy; center, double orange poppy; right, white lily; RSG Marks 10 (left and right) and 11 (center).*

Plate 337. *Humidor, 8"h, RSP Mold 631 (Medallion Mold); Embossed Star Decoration "c" (see Ambiguous Marks); wide black borders with gold stencilled designs; RSG Mark 9.*

Plate 338. *Jam Jar with Underplate; orange tinted roses with shadow flowers; RSG Mark 11 without "Handpainted."*

Plate 340. *Mustard Pot, 3"h; pink and white roses; gold highlights; RSG Mark 7 without red script mark.*

Plate 339. *Mustard Pot, 3½"h, RSP Mold 502; butterscotch finish with wide gold border and trim; RSG Mark 9.*

Plate 341. *Mustard Pot, 3½"h; large blue tinted flowers; gold trim; RSG Mark 7.*

Plate 342. *Mustard Pot, 3⅛"h, with ladle, 4¼"l; white tulips; RSG Mark 8.*

Plate 343. *Salt Dips (or possibly Egg Cups), 1"h x 1¾"d; pedestal base; cream border decorated with orange roses and gold stencilled leaves; RSG Mark 9.*

Plate 344. *Set of Salt Dips, 3" x 2½"; gold roses and leaves on ivory background; RSG Mark 12.*

Plate 345. *Footed Salt Dips (or Nut Cups), 1½" x 3¼"; white flowers with gold stencilled designs; RSG Mark 8.*

Plate 346. *Salt Dip, 4½"l, pierced handle; white lily; gold border; RSG Mark 7.*

Plate 347. *Salt Dip, 3"l; pink and white lilies; shaded green background; gold trim; RSG Mark 9.*

Plate 348. *High Top Shoe; large yellow rose on toe with a cluster of pink flowers on side; cream background; RSG Mark 10.*

Plate 349. *Syrup Pitcher, 3½"h; light yellow roses; gold tapestry design at top of pitcher; RSG Mark 8.*

Plate 350. *Syrup Pitcher, 4"h, and Underplate, hexagon shape mold (pitcher); white and orange flowers; gold trim; RSG Mark 11 without "Handpainted."*

Plate 351. *Tankard, 13¾"h, RSP Mold 537; bronze and orange mums; RSG Mark.*

Plate 352. *Teapot, 4¼"h; yellow and orange tinted roses; gold stencilled designs on borders; RSG Mark 8.*

Plate 353. Tea Set: Creamer, 2¾"h; Teapot, 4½"h; Covered Sugar Bowl, 3¾"h; RSP Mold 475; RSP FD97, Dogwood and Pine decor on body with a white leaf composing border design; gold trim; RSG Mark 7.

Plate 354. Toothbrush Holder, 4¼"l; pink rose on tinted blue-green background; RSG Mark 9.

Plate 355. Toothpick Holder, 3 handles; white floral design; tinted green leaves; gold trim; RSG Mark 9.

113

Plate 356. Vase, 5½"h, R.S. Suhl Mold 10; yellow daffodils; pearl luster finish; RSG Mark 11 without "Handpainted."

Plate 357. Vase, 5¾"h; figural decor based on scene from Rembrandt's "Night Watch"; red finish on borders; gold trim; RSG Mark 10 with "Naohbuache, Rembrandt" written in gold script. (This is a different scene from the ones shown in Plates 553 and 554 of the Second Series.)

Plate 358. Vase, 4"h, RSP Mold 909; salesman's sample; Windmill scenic decor (a different transfer from the one shown in Plate 627 in the Second Series); RSG Mark 9.

Plate 359. Pair of Vases, 5½"h; white lilies on shaded brown background; RSG Mark 9.

Plate 360. *Vase, 8¼"h, R.S. Suhl Mold 3; pink peonies and snowballs; RSG Mark 9 without "Germany."*

Plate 361. *Pair of Vases, 5⅛"h; hand-painted white and pink roses, artist signed "C.F. Wyatt" (non-factory decoration); RSG Mark 10.*

Plate 362. *Vase, 13"h; Peace Bringing Plenty figural decor; red finish on top border; gold stencilled designs; RSG Mark 4, rare marked example.*

R.S. Tillowitz and R.S. Silesia

There are several versions of the R.S. Tillowitz mark. Two of those marks are not found on china which was exported to America. RST Mark 1 consists of the initials arranged vertically within an oval composed of dots. A tile with this mark was photostated by Mr. Capers when he visited the current PT Factory in Poland. A copy of that is shown in an Appendix. This particular mark is noted as having been registered in 1916 (Danckert, 1984: 476).

Mark 2 includes the RS initials with a fancy "T" in script form. One example of a vase, found in Germany, is shown with the photographs. Röntgen (1980: 347) lists this mark in use after 1932 until 1938.

The other RST marks are similar to the RSG wreath marks. They include the word "Tillowitz" instead of Germany and are found in several colors. Mark 6 is the RST mark most commonly found in this country. In addition to Tillowitz, "Silesia" is written in script form below the mark.

Mark 5 is often found as a double mark with the RST marks, and it can be found as a single mark. The letters "EPOS" translate to "Fine Porcelain from Upper Silesia."

RST Mark 8 was first shown in G2 (old Mark 50). The RST wreath is at the base of this rather elaborate mark. No additional examples of this mark have been found.

Marks 9, 10, and 11 are R.S. Silesia marks. They are also wreath marks. "Royal" has been added to the mark in RSS Mark 11. Mark 12 is actually a porcelain advertising sign incorporating the R.S. Tillowitz mark.

Most of the china pictured in this section was discovered by Mr. Capers in Germany. These marks, used during the 1930s and 1940s, represent a time when little china was exported from Germany to the United States. Some of the decoration also reflects the floral styles popular during those pre-World War II years. Other pieces are decorated with the same stylized floral decor associated with the RSG marks. A few unmarked examples are included under the RST marks because they seem to fit into that category.

Several items with the RST marks are shown in an Appendix in addition to the tile mentioned above. These represent some of the figurines manufactured by the Tillowitz factory. The Tillowitz figures are rarely found in this country, although one is shown by Clifford Schlegelmilch (1970: 35).

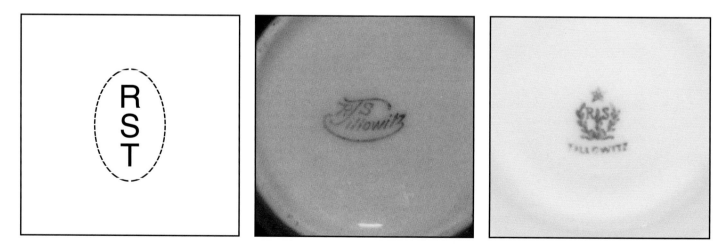

R.S. Tillowitz Mark 1, initials arranged vertically in a dotted circle.

R.S. Tillowitz Mark 2, green script mark.

R.S. Tillowitz Mark 3, wreath mark in green, blue, or brown.

R.S. Tillowitz Mark 4, wreath mark in brown, blue, or green with "EPOS" (Fine Porcelain from Upper Silesia).

R.S. Tillowitz Mark 5, "EPOS" mark in green with "Echt Eifenbein-Porzellan" (fine ivory porcelain).

R.S. Tillowitz Mark 6, blue wreath mark with "Tillowitz, Silesia"; "Germany, Handpainted" in green.

R.S. Tillowitz Mark 7, this wreath mark can be found in blue, green, or black.

R.S. Tillowitz Mark 8, figural mark of a woman with a bow and pattern name "Diana" with the R.S. Tillowitz wreath mark.

R.S. Silesia Mark 9, wreath mark in green or blue.

R.S. Silesia Mark 10, uncolored wreath mark.

R.S. Silesia Mark 11, green wreath mark with "Royal" printed above wreath.

R.S. Tillowitz Mark 12, porcelain advertising sign incorporating wreath mark and "EPOS."

Plate 363. *Vase, 4⅜"h, salesman's sample; pink and yellow tinted roses; RST Mark 2.*

Plate 364. *Coffee Set: Covered Sugar Bowl, Coffee Pot, and Creamer; small red-orange floral pattern; RST Mark 5.*

Plate 365. *Cake Plate, 10⅞"d; RSP Fruit V decor, pears with grapes; RST Mark 3 in blue.*

Plate 366. *One Handled Dish, 10¾"d, RSP Mold 181; pink and white roses; RST Mark 3 in green.*

118

Plate 367. *One Handled Dish, 7⅜"d, RSP Mold 181; small clusters of multicolored flowers in center and around inner border; RST Mark 4 in brown.*

Plate 368. *One Handled Dish, 7½"d, RSP Mold 181; pink roses with other flowers scattered around inner border; gold stencilled designs; gold trim; RST Mark 4 in green.*

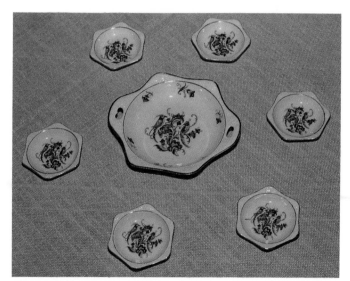

Plate 369. *Dessert Set: Master Bowl, 7⅝"d; Individual Bowls, 3⅝"d; bird and floral pattern in shades of gold and blue; variations of RST Mark 4 in blue and in green.*

Plate 370. *Berry Bowls, 3"d; same bird and floral pattern as in Plate 369; RST Mark 4 in blue.*

Plate 371. *Berry or Condiment Bowls, 3⅝"d; fancy floral and leaf design in shades of blue; RST Mark 4 in green.*

Plate 372. *Two Handled Dish, 7⅜"d; multicolored flowers connected by a floral chain forms pattern; gold stencilled designs around inner border; gold trim; RST Mark 4 in green.*

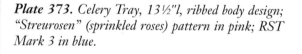

Plate 373. *Celery Tray, 13½"l, ribbed body design; "Streurosen" (sprinkled roses) pattern in pink; RST Mark 3 in blue.*

Plate 374. *Covered Sugar Bowl and Cup and Saucer in the same pink rose pattern shown in Plate 373; thin gold trim; RST Mark 3 in blue.*

Plate 375. Coffee Pot, 8¾"h; Creamer, 4¾"h; Covered Sugar Bowl, 4⅜"h; "China Blau" (blue china) pattern; RST Mark 3 in green. This and the following three pictures are of pieces from a Dinner Service.

Plate 376. Cup (left), 2⅛"h x 3⅜"d; Cup (right), 2½"h x 3"d; "China Blau" pattern; RST Mark 3 in green.

Plate 377. Covered Butter Dish, 3¾"h x 6⅝"d; "China Blau" pattern; RST Mark 3 in green.

Plate 378. Two Handled Bowl, 10½" x 9½"; "China Blau" pattern; RST Mark 3 in green.

121

Plate 379. Plates from a Dinner Service, 7⅝"d; floral bouquets decorate center and inner border; each plate has a different multicolored floral design; RST Mark 4 in green with "1931" indicating the year of production.

Plate 380. Cup, 4"h, and Saucer; Plate 7¾"d; large pink rose with a blue flower forms pattern in center and around inner border; fancy gold scrolled and stencilled work around border; RST Mark 4 in green.

Plate 381. Coffee Pot, 8½"h; ribbed body design painted yellow on alternating sections to form a striped pattern; R.S. Silesia, Mark 9.

Plate 382. Vase, two handled, Art Deco style mold; red finish on base, inner border, and on balls on handles; RST Mark 3 in green.

122

Plate 383. Cup, 2¼"h, and Saucer; Plate, 7⅝"d; red-orange finish forms wide inner borders; gold stencilled floral and scrolled designs around outer borders; RST Mark 3 in green with "Handerbeit" (Handpainted) in red.

Plate 384. Ginger Jar, 9"h; cobalt blue and gold floral design on reserves around top of jar; cobalt blue finish on body and lid; gold trim; RST Mark 5 in green.

Plate 385. Pair of Vases, 7⅛"h; large white flowers and leaves outlined against a dark cobalt blue background; RST Mark 4 in brown.

123

Plate 386. Cheese Dish, 2⅜"h, 8⅝"d (base), 4⅝"d (top tier); large yellow tinted roses on shaded brown background; RST Mark 7 in blue.

Plate 387. Chop Plate, 11"d; large yellow tinted roses on shaded brown background; RST Mark 7 in blue.

Plate 388. Cake Plate, 9¾"d; coral fuschias with shadow leaves; RST Mark 7 in blue.

Plate 389. Cake Plate, 9½"d; white lilies; RST Mark 7 in blue.

Plate 390. Cake Plate, 10"d; red poinsettias; RST Mark 6.

Plate 391. Two Handled Dish, 7½"w; pink roses on shaded green background; R.S. Silesia, Mark 10.

Plate 392. *Gravy Boat, 6½"l; pink roses decorate interior; RST Mark 6.*

Plate 393. *Plate; pink and white single tulips around outer border; RST Mark 6.*

Plate 394. *Covered Sugar Bowl, 3¾"h; large white flowers with gold highlights; RST Mark 6.*

Plate 395. *Covered Sugar Bowl, 3½"h; yellow daffodils; RST Mark 7 in blue.*

126

Plate 396. Tray, 13½"l x 4½"w; pink tinted lilies; RST Mark 7 in black.

Plate 397. Cup, 1¾"h, and Saucer; white petaled flowers with large yellow centers; RST Mark 7 in blue.

Plate 398. Egg Cups, 2¼"h; Tray, 7¾"l x 4⅛"w; ribbed body design; gold trim; marked "Tillowitz" in blue.

Plate 399. Covered Sugar Bowl, 4"h, and Creamer, 3"h; orange poppies and white water lily on dark cobalt blue background around top half of pieces; gold finish with engraved designs on base; RST Mark 6.

Plate 400. *Two Handled Bowl, 6¾"d; pink, peach, and white flowers; gold tapestry designs on gray-blue background; RST Mark 6.*

Plate 401. *Plate, 6¼"d; pink, peach, and white floral pattern as in Plate 400; R.S. Silesia Mark 9 in green.*

Plate 402. *Cake Set; clusters of pink roses with shadow leaves; RST Mark 6.*

Plate 403. *Bowl, 8"sq; same rose pattern as in Plate 402; unmarked.*

Plate 404. *Cracker Jar; lavender flowers decorate gold center border; semi-gloss finish; RST Mark 7 in blue with artist's signature "B.S. Rodgers," signed on bottom in green (non-factory decoration).*

Plate 405. *Powder Box, 2¾"h, and Hair Receiver, 2¼"h; white flowers on cream to green background; gold stencilled designs; RST Mark 7 in blue.*

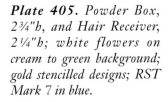

Plate 406. *Vase, 4⅜"h, salesman's sample; peach and yellow tinted roses; RST Mark 3 in green.*

Plate 407. *Vase 4⅞"h, salesman's sample; white and lavender flowers; RST Mark 3 in green.*

Plate 408. *Tray, 11"l x 8"w; roses decorate center and four corners of tray; blue design on outer border; RST Mark 7 in black.*

Plate 409. *Oval Two Handled Dish, 9¾"l x 4¾"w; pink lilies; R.S. Tillowitz wreath mark.*

Plate 410. *Relish, 8"l x 3¾"w; Lily of the Valley; tan border; gold trim; R.S. Silesia Mark 10.*

Plate 411. *One Handled Plate, Lemon Dish, or Nappy, 6½"d; coral fuschias with large green leaves; R.S. Silesia Mark 11.*

Plate 412. *Vase, 3⅛"h, salesman's sample; light and dark pink roses around top border on black background; gold trim; unmarked.*

Plate 413. *Vase, 6¼"h; large pink tinted flower with smaller orange flowers on brown toned background; unmarked.*

R.S. Wing Mark

The R.S. Wing mark is perhaps the most elaborate or artistic of the various R.S. marks. No reference documents a precise time for the mark, but the pre-World War I era is probably the most logical time frame. Few examples are found with this distinctive mark. The molds are more similar to Steeple marked china than to any other R.S. marked china. The decoration is usually in the form of pastel floral designs. These may incorporate a combination of transfer and hand-painted work.

R.S. Wing and Star Mark with "Germany" in brown or reddish brown.

Plate 414. *Plate, 9¼"d; multicolored daisies; tinted pink border; R.S. Germany Wing Mark.*

Plate 415. *Covered Box, 4⅛"l, heart shaped with molded hair pin on lid; hand-painted small multicolored flowers; gold highlights; light green finish; R.S. Germany Wing Mark.*

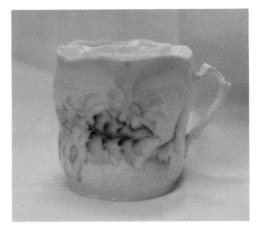

Plate 416. Shaving Mug, 3½"h; hand-painted pink flowers on light green background; R.S. Germany Wing Mark.

Plate 417. Smoking Set, 9¼"l x 5"w; red roses with blue highlights; gold trim; unmarked (mold has been verified with the R.S. Germany Wing Mark).

Plate 417a. Smoking Set, 8"l; small pink rose garlands; unmarked.

Plate 419. Cup, 2¼"h, and Saucer; blue floral pattern; gold trim; R.S. Germany Wing Mark.

Plate 418. Chocolate Pot, 8"h; pastel floral spray; gold trim; R.S. Germany Wing Mark.

Plate 420. Covered Sugar Bowl; embossed leaf designs on body; R.S. Germany Wing Mark.

Molded "RS" Marks

Two versions of molded or embossed "RS" marks are shown here. The marks only consist of the two initials. These marks are on two covered boxes and a hair receiver. This mark with the RSP mark is also found on an example in the *Third Series* (see Plate 498). Plate 514 in that edition has only the molded mark. Those two examples were included under the R.S. Prussia mark in order to introduce RSP Mold Numbers for the pieces.

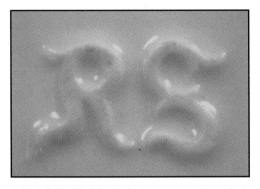

Molded "RS" Mark 1. This type of mark is actually an applied mark, formed by making the letters with liquid slip (clay mixture) similar to cake decorating.

Molded "RS" Mark 2. Letters vary slightly from Mark 1.

Plate 421. *Covered Box, 4"d, a leaf type mold; lavender finish; Molded "RS" Mark 1.*

Plate 422. *Covered Box, 4"d; pink finish; Molded "RS" Mark 1.*

Plate 423. *Hair Receiver, 4¼"d, RSP Mold 40; pink and white mums; Molded "RS" Mark 2.*

135

R.S. Germany Double Marks

Like the RSP mark, the RSG wreath mark is sometimes found with a "Royal" mark which cannot be explained. The double marks are usually on an identified RSP or RSG mold. A few of those marks are shown here.

Another interesting mark was found with the RST wreath mark. It is similar to the RSG Gold script mark. The initials "E & R" and "Handpainted" are stamped in gold. Could this possibly be a mark for Erdmann and Reinhold?

Hartwich (1984: 15) mentions that the E.S. factory and other "local" factories (that is, the R.S. factory) organized a class in the Oberlaender school in 1904, for the purpose of instructing china painters. Could this "E & R" mark have been used by students in the class? The mark certainly appears to be a decorator's mark.

The example with the mark also has the appearance of professional decoration consistent with factory decoration (as opposed to work by a professional china painter who decorated blanks for a decorating studio, such as Pickard). Perhaps future research will bring forth information on this particular mark.

The Friedrich II mark was shown in G2. It is found as a single mark or with the RSG wreath mark. Like the "Royal" marks, the reason for its use is not know. Molds and decoration have RSG characteristics. An example has been found double marked with the green R.S. Suhl wreath mark. This could indicate the Friedrich II mark was used prior to 1917. The mark, however, could also have been added at a later time to the R.S. Suhl marked piece.

R.S. Germany Wreath Mark with "Royal Cologne."

Plate 424. *Plate, 6¼"d; white tulips; RSG Mark with "Royal Cologne" mark.*

R.S. Germany Wreath Mark with "Royal Nürnburg."

Royal Nürnburg Mark with "Germany" in blue and "Handpainted" script mark.

Plate 425. Berry Set, Master Bowl, 9"d and Individual Bowls, 5"d; RSP Mold 256; surreal flowers on shaded brown background; luster finish; RSG Mark with "Royal Nürnburg" on Master Bowl; "Royal Nürnburg" with "Germany" on Individual Bowls.

Plate 426. Cake Plate, 10"d; white and orange tulips on tinted green background; RSG Wreath Mark 7 with "Royal Erfurt." (See "Royal Erfurt" Mark in photograph preceding Plate 551).

R.S. Germany Wreath Mark with "E & R, Handpainted" in gold script.

Plate 427. *Cheese Dish, 4"h, 9"d, two tiers; pink lilies on shaded green background; RSG Mark with "E & R" Mark.*

R.S. Germany Wreath Mark with "Friedrich II" Mark in gold.

Friedrich II Mark without RSG Mark.

Plate 428. *Two Handled Dish, 6½"d; coral and white poppies; gold stencilled designs; gold trim; Friedrich II Mark without RSG Mark.*

R.S. Poland

The R.S. (Made in German Poland) mark is found as a double mark with the R.S. Germany mark or "Germany" or as a single mark on china. The mark was not used until after 1945. It was probably discontinued sometime during the late 1940s or early 1950s. It was not used after 1956. At that time, a new wreath mark with the initials "P.T." and "Tulowice, Made in Poland" was implemented (Chroscicki, 1974: 76). It should be noted, however, that the PT mark may have been used a few years prior to the date (1956) Chroscicki lists. This mark, like most of the RS marks, cannot be dated precisely.

The R.S. Poland mark is usually found on molds and with decorations common to other RS marked china. Many of the pieces shown here are proof that the R.S. Poland mark was simply added to old stock. The same is true for the R.S. Poland marked china shown in G1 and G2. The two cups and saucers shown in the first two photographs in this section, however, appear to be new stock made after 1945.

The last two photographs represent the production of the Polish owned factory after circa 1956. Other material relating to that factory which is still in operation can be found in an Appendix in the *Third Series*.

R.S. Poland Mark with blue RSG Wreath Mark and "Handpainted." (Mark may not have RSG wreath or "Handpainted.")

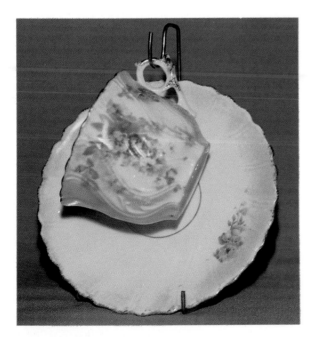

Plate 429. Cup, 2½"h, and Saucer; small pink flowers; R.S. Poland Mark.

Plate 430. Cup, 2½"h, and Saucer; pink rose with a yellow and white daisy on light blue background; R.S. Poland Mark.

Plate 431. Chocolate Cup, 3"h, RSP Mold 509a; RSP FD97, Dogwood and Pine decor; iridescent finish; R.S. Poland Mark.

Plate 432. Ewer, 5½"h, RSG Mold; Windmill scenic decor (RSG transfer); R.S. Poland Mark.

Plate 433. Pair of Vases, 5⅞"h, RSP Mold 907 (and R.S. Suhl Mold 16); RSP FD39, lilac clematis; R.S. Poland Mark.

Plate 434. Vase, 5¼"h, salesman's sample; Reapers figural decor with two women in long dresses; R.S. Poland Mark .

Plate 435. *Pair of Vases, 8½"h, R.S. Suhl Mold 3; woman figural pastoral scene; cobalt blue finish on base; gold trim; R.S. Poland Mark.*

Plate 436. *Pair of Vases, 7½"h; orange tinted roses; wide gold band around top part of vases; R.S. Poland Mark.*

Plate 437. *Vase, 4⅜"h, salesman's sample; large pink tinted flower on shaded brown background; R.S. Poland Mark.*

Plate 438. *Ewer, 6¼"h, RSP Mold 900; Night Watch figural scene after Rembrandt; dark green finish; R.S. Poland Mark.*

Plate 439. *Vase, 6"h; RSG Sheepherder figural and scenic decor (houses vary in background); R.S. Poland Mark.*

Plate 440. *Vase, 6"h; Sheepherder decor as in Plate 439, but house is different; R.S. Poland Mark.*

Plate 441. Vase, 9"h, R.S. Suhl Mold 15; Chinese Pheasants; R.S. Poland Mark, rare marked example.

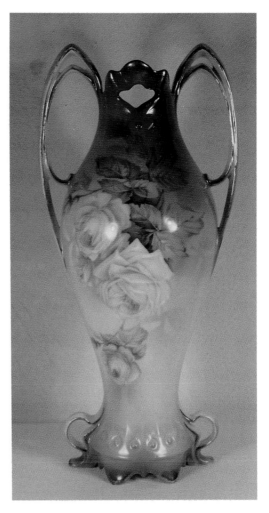

Plate 442. Vase, 12"h, Art Nouveau shaped handles, RSP Mold 956; large peach roses on shaded brown background; R.S. Poland Mark.

P.T. Poland Wreath and Star Mark in brown; current mark used by the Polish owned factory. (P.T. Tulowice, Made in Poland.)

Plate 443. Coffee Service: Pot, Cups and Saucers, Creamer and Covered Sugar Bowl; gold spattered or marbled finish; P.T. Poland Mark.

Ambiguous Marks and Photographs
Embossed Star Marks
Saxe Altenburg
Royal Vienna
Other Royal and Red Crown Marks
Other Ambiguous Marks

Often, examples of china are attributed to one of the Schlegelmilch factories even though the piece does not have a printed Schlegelmilch mark. Based on the shape or mold of the china as well as the decoration, the piece seems to have the characteristics associated with Schlegelmilch porcelain. Such china may be unmarked, or it may have what can be called an "ambiguous" mark. An ambiguous mark is one which cannot be attributed definitely to a specific factory. Embossed star marks, the Saxe Altenburg mark, printed crown marks, and "Royal" marks such as "Royal Vienna" are some examples of ambiguous marks. Just when and by whom such marks were used is not known. There is some sort of "link" however, between those marks and Schlegelmilch china. Sometimes these marks are found with RS Prussia or RS Germany marks. This double marking has caused collectors to consider pieces so marked, even if the mark is not combined with an RS mark, as "Prussia."

This section of the book is designed as a study segment for collectors. Because Schlegelmilch china seems to be collected on a wider basis each year, more and more examples are appearing on the market. It is now possible to begin a serious examination of some of these ambiguous marks which have puzzled collectors for years. By grouping china with these marks into a special section, perhaps it will be possible to see that while many pieces do share a certain mold or decoration with Schlegelmilch marked china, they also have their own unique characteristics.

Various ambiguous marks are shown with photographs of china with those marks. Notations have been made to point out the characteristics which the pieces have in common with RS marked china. Although all of the available references on Schlegelmilch china have been studied to compare mold, marks, and decorations, it is indeed possible that some examples will be found which will not agree with my conclusions. I will be glad to hear from collectors who have substantiating, new, or different information.

The relatively few examples of china which are found with these ambiguous marks in comparison to the amount of marked Schlegelmilch china suggest that the china was not intended for export to America or that the marks were used by a factory with little production. Some other interpretations of the marks could be that small factories copied certain Schlegelmilch molds and decorations and added their own marks, or some factories or decorating firms purchased Schlegelmilch blanks (undecorated china) and used the same or similar decorations, adding their own special mark.

Another interesting possibility is that the molds and decorations were copied not by German factories but by Japanese factories. The Japanese competition for the American ceramic market after 1891, is noted by Hartwich (1984: 13, 14). The Japanese were not only said to be a competitor producing china, but they were also said to be duplicating ES molds, causing the company to change its production. It is important for collectors to realize that no one china factory had a monopoly on certain decoration transfers. It also would not have been difficult to copy molds, especially some of the simpler ones.

Some of the most highly decorated china and elaborately molded items are found with these ambiguous marks. The value of the pieces should be judged according to that criteria, rather than the particular mark which is on the piece. This is certainly true for china made during the same time period as RS marked china and which also represents a fine quality. But not all of the china with ambiguous marks can be compared favorably in quality to Schlegelmilch porcelain.

Although most of the ambiguously marked china seems to have more in common with the RS marked porcelain, there are also a few ambiguous marks, molds, and decorations which seem to relate more to the ES factory. Those examples are included under the Erdmann Schlegelmilch Company.

Embossed Star Marks

In Hayden's monograph (1970: 3), a "star" mark was described as being the "oldest" mark on R.S. Prussia china. The author lists no references, and he does not give any basis for his statement. No factual information has been found which substantiates that statement. I discussed in my first edition that while star marks may sometimes be found with an RSP mark as well, such marks alone cannot be definitely attributed to Schlegelmilch factories (Gaston, 1986: 25). Because those marks were shown, however, it seems that many collectors have only looked at the pictures of the marks and have not read the material preceding those pictures. Many continue to consider any embossed star (or other raised mark such as a "circle" mold mark) on a piece of china as synonymous with an R.S. Prussia mark.

From studying quite a number of examples with embossed star marks, however, it is clear that the tie between those marks and Schlegelmilch china is really limited to a few molds and to a few decorations. Other molds and decorations with these star marks fall into a definite "star" category of china. The examples shown here are only marked with one of the embossed star marks. They do not have an additional RSP mark. One example which had both the star mark and an RSP mark is shown under R.S. Prussia china in the *Third Series*. (See Plate 508.) Another example which has an embossed star mark and an R.S. Germany mark is shown in Plate 283 in this edition. That piece is a covered box in a leaf shaped mold (RSP Mold 834). Three other examples of that mold are shown in this section because they were marked with only an embossed star.

Two versions of the embossed star mark are shown here. Star Mark 1 has six points while Star Mark 2 has eight points. These two embossed marks are the only ones of this type shown in this *Fourth Series*. A few pictures were sent by collectors of an embossed "cross" mark similar to Mark 14 in G1 and G2, but it was not the same. The shape was more defined. Neither the objects, molds, or decorations on those pieces matched any Schlegelmilch marked piece or any of the other ambiguous marks. Old Mark 14 also has been deleted from this book because of lack of examples which fit Schlegelmilch characteristics.

I have used the term "star" with lower case letters "a" through "j" to identify specific floral decorations found on china which has a star mark. Star decorations "a" through "d" are the ones most often seen. A few of the star marked items have a Steeple floral decoration. Unmarked china which is decorated with a star floral pattern has been included here as well.

The popular Hidden Image mold has been placed in this section. The Hidden Image Molds (old RSP Mold numbered 4, 5, 515, and 827) are found either unmarked, or with an embossed Star mark, or in some cases with a Saxe Altenburg mark. No authentic RSP marked example of the Hidden Image mold has been found. While the Hidden Image mold can be found with a Saxe Altenburg mark as noted in G2 (p. 26), the mold has not been placed in the Saxe Altenburg section for two reasons. First, the Star mark is molded into the china and represents a mark made as the piece was formed. The Saxe Altenburg mark is printed and could have been added at any time by any factory. Although the Star marks and the Saxe Altenburg marks may be from the same factory, that cannot be proven at this time. Second, no Hidden Image examples with the Saxe Altenburg mark were available to include in this edition. The photographs of the Hidden Image mold shown here have either Star or Steeple decorations. The pieces are marked only with an embossed star or, they are unmarked.

Old RSP Mold 6 in G1 was also a type of Hidden Image mold. A house rather than a woman's cameo was made in the mold. That particular mold was moved to the Steeple section, however, because a Steeple marked example was found. The piece shown in G1 had been unmarked.

A page from an old catalog shown in Lehr and Follett's book (1964) shows some pieces of china with the Hidden Image. The Hidden Image is referred to as "cameo" or "Floradora." Unfortunately, the advertisement does not indicate the name of any factory associated with manufacturing the pieces.

Following the Star marked pieces, several unmarked examples of the Hidden Image Mold are shown as well as a few other unmarked molds with a star decoration. Unmarked Steeple Molds 8 and 12, and unmarked RSP Molds 343, 502, 834, and 664 with Star decorations are in this section.

To conclude discussion on embossed Star marked china, we find that only a few Schlegelmilch molds are found with such marks. In some cases, the decorations on Star marked china overlap with RSP and Steeple transfers. Decorations unique to the Star marks, however, are more prevalent. Star decorations are found on unmarked china as well. This leads to the conclusion that such unmarked pieces were also probably made by whatever factory was responsible for using the embossed Star marks.

Embossed Star Mark 1, 6 point star.

Embossed Star Mark 2, 8 point star.

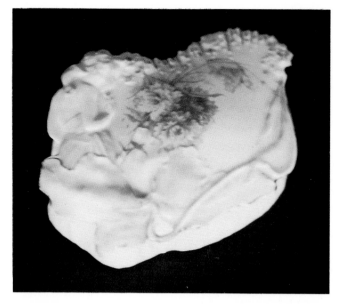

Plate 444. *Covered Box, 7" x 5", Hidden Image Mold; Star Floral Decoration "a" (FDa), a pink, a yellow, and a white mum. Note that the image is almost the full back figure of a woman dressed in a strapless gown. The style of this figure and the dress suggest a time period later than the Victorian era. Star Mark 1.*

Plate 445. *Creamer, 3"h, companion to RSP Mold 343 (Steeple Mold 8); Star FDb, cluster of small multicolored flowers; dark green background with gold stencilled designs; Star Mark 1.*

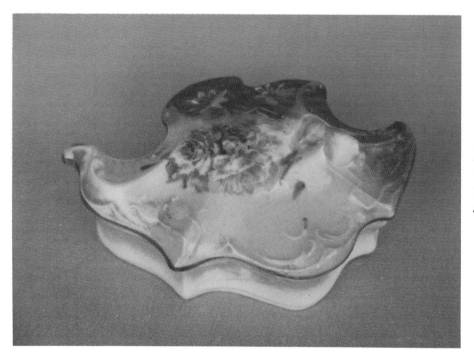

Plate 446. *Covered Box, 4¼" x 3"; Star FDc, cluster of yellow and pink roses; shaded dark to light green background; Star Mark 1.*

Plate 447. *Toothpick Holder; Star FDd, three white asters; tinted green background; Star Mark 1.*

Plate 448. *Mush or Oatmeal Set: Milk Jug, 4"h; Bowl, 6"d; Plate, 9"d; companion to RSP Mold 343 (Steeple Mold 8); Steeple FDR, large yellow flower with smaller blue, pink, and white flowers; rust colored background overlaid with shadow flowers; Star Mark 1.*

Plate 449. *Hair Receiver, 5"l, Hidden Image Mold, woman's cameo with hair piled high on head; tinted pink flowers; blue-green highlights with shadow flowers; hair painted gold; Star Mark 1.*

Plate 458. Covered Sugar Bowl, 5"h and Teapot, 6½"h; Star FDi, small yellow and orange flowers with enameled work; gold trim; Star Mark 1.

Plate 459. Covered Sugar Bowl, 5"h; Star FDj, two pink roses with one white and one yellow rose; blue highlights; Star Mark 1.

Plate 460. Covered Sugar Bowl, 4¼"h, companion to RSP Mold 343 (Steeple Mold 8); Star FDc, pink and yellow roses; Star Mark 2.

Plate 461. Creamer, 3¾"h and Teapot, 5"h, companion to RSP Mold 343 (Steeple Mold 8); Star FDa, pink, yellow, and white mums; Star Mark 2.

Plate 462. Cracker Jar, 7¼"h, companion to RSP Mold 343 (Steeple Mold 8); Steeple FDC, large white flowers with large green leaves; Steeple BG2, cobalt blue border with white flowers; Star Mark 2.

Plate 463. Pitcher, 7½"h, Hidden Image Mold on back and front; Star Mark 2.

Plate 464. *Pin Tray, 7"l x 5½"w, Hidden Image Mold, woman's cameo with ribbon in hair; Star FDa, pink, yellow, and white mums; pink highlights; green hair; unmarked.*

Plate 465. *Cake Plate, Hidden Image Mold, woman's profile with long hair; Star FDa, pink finish on border; green hair. (This particular example had an RSP wreath mark which was determined not to be authentic.)*

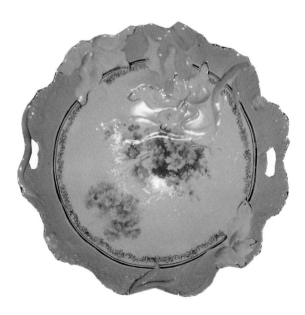

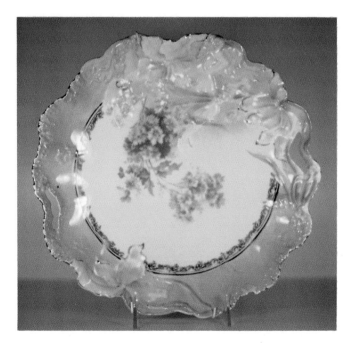

Plate 466. *Cake Plate, 11"d, Hidden Image Mold, woman's cameo; Star FDb, small multicolored flowers; blue border; gold stencilled pattern around inner border; unmarked.*

Plate 467. *Cake Plate, 11"d, Hidden Image Mold; frontal view of woman's face and shoulders; Star FDb; blue border; gold stencilled pattern around inner border; unmarked.*

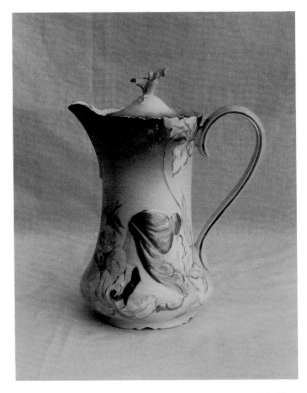

Plate 468. Chocolate Pot, 9"h, Hidden Image Mold on front and back (gold hair on front; green hair on back); unmarked.

Plate 469. Bowl, 9½"d, pierced handles, Hidden Image Mold; Steeple FDQ, a pink, a yellow, and a white mum; (this decoration is very similar to Star FDa, but it is not the same); green border; unmarked.

Plate 470. Cake Plate, 12"d, Hidden Image Mold, two cameos; Steeple FDQ; rose finish on border; iridescent bronze hair; unmarked.

Plate 471. Cup, 2¼"h, and Saucer, Hidden Image Mold; Steeple FDQ; blue border; gold trim; hair painted gold; unmarked.

155

Plate 472. Dresser Tray, 11"l x 7"w; Hidden Image Mold, two cameos (different from the two faces in Plate 470); Steeple FDQ; light green finish; unmarked.

Plate 473. Bowl, 10"d; Hidden Image Mold, woman's cameo with long brown curls and a floral transfer decoration worked into hair; Steeple FDQ in center of bowl; blue border with shadow flowers; gold stencilled inner border; unmarked.

Plate 474. Bowl, 12"l x 10¼"w, Hidden Image Mold; Steeple FDQ; cobalt blue inner border; border; gold outlining on molded flowers around outer border; gold beaded rim; back of bowl also has molded scroll work; unmarked.

Plate 475. Tea Set: Covered Sugar Bowl, 5"h; Teapot, 6"h; Creamer, 4"h; RSP Mold 502; Star FDj, two pink roses with one white and one yellow rose; unmarked.

Plate 476. *Cup, 2⅝"h, and Saucer, RSP Mold 502; Star FDd, white asters; lavender finish on border; unmarked.*

Plate 477. *Syrup Pitcher, 5½"h, RSP Mold 502; Star FDd, white asters; green finish on borders; unmarked.*

Plate 478. *Pitcher, 7½"h, RSP Mold 502; Star FDd, white asters; blue-green finish on top border; light green finish on body; unmarked.*

Plate 479. *Chocolate Pot, 9"h (lid missing), RSP Mold 502; Star FDd, white asters; pink finish on top border; blue finish on base; unmarked.*

Plate 480. Bowl, 10¾"d; free form shape with beaded edge; Star FDa, pink, yellow, and white roses; cobalt blue inner border and highlights around outer border, all overlaid with gold stencilled floral designs; unmarked.

Plate 481. Plate, 10¼"d; fancy pierced work incorporating floral designs; beaded rim; Star FDa; rose finish on dome shapes around inner border; unmarked.

Plate 482. Bowl, 10¼"d, mold match to Plate 481 except border does not have the pierced work; Star FDc, pink and yellow roses; rose finish on dome shapes around inner border; unmarked.

Plate 483. Bowl, 9"d; Star FDc, blue-green finish on border with shadow flowers; unmarked.

Plate 484. Candle Holder, 3¼"h; Star FDd, white asters; unmarked.

Plate 485. Chocolate Pot, 9½"h, companion to RSP Mold 343 (Steeple Mold 8); Star FDa, small multicolored flowers; green border with shadow flowers; gold stencilled designs; gold trim; unmarked.

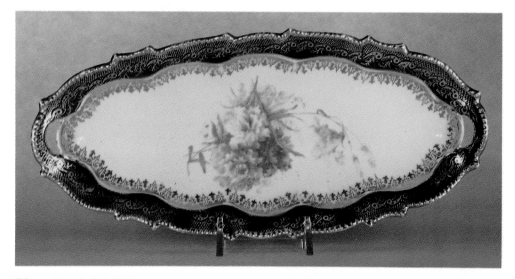

Plate 486. *Relish Dish, 9½"l x 4¼"w, RSP Mold 343 (Steeple Mold 8); Star FDa, pink, yellow, and white mums; dark green outer border with gold stencilled work on outer and inner borders; gold trim; unmarked.*

Plate 487. *Coffee Set: Covered Sugar Bowl, 6½"h; Coffee Pot, 8"h; Creamer, 5½"h; Steeple Mold 12; Star FDa, pink, yellow, and white mums on creamer and sugar bowl; Steeple FDU, large yellow rose with smaller pink rose, on Coffee Pot; shaded pink finish; gold trim; unmarked.*

Plate 488. *Punch Cups or Water Tumblers, 4¼"h x 3¼"d, RSP Mold 664 (Steeple Mold 12); Star FDa; light green finish; unmarked.*

160

Saxe Altenburg

The Saxe Altenburg marks are ambiguous because the marks have not been definitely documented for a particular china factory. Some of the molds and decorations, however, are the same or similar to china made by the Schlegelmilch factories. A mark similar to the Saxe Altenburg Crown mark (see Saxe Altenburg Mark 2) is shown by Röntgen (1980: 92) as well as several other references on marks. The mark is attributed to Unger & Schilde who operated a porcelain factory in the town of Roschütz from 1881. This location was also in Thuringia, like the E.S. and R.S. Schlegelmilch factories. The mark is noted as being used from circa 1906. This time, of course, coincides with when the Schlegelmilch factories were in production.

The mark, however, is not the same as the ones shown here. The wording is a little different although a "crown" does make up part of the mark. The mark Röntgen shows (p. 92) has the words "Altenburg Saxony" printed beneath a Crown flanked on each side by a leafy branch. The entire mark is enclosed in a circle. The Saxe Altenburg Marks shown here are printed in red. The stamp appears rather crude. Mark 2 also incorporates a "Crown" with the words "Saxe Altenburg."

These Saxe Altenburg Marks are sometimes found on documented Schlegelmilch molds. Decorations associated with Schlegelmilch marked china also may be found with the Saxe Altenburg mark. Two studies relating to this topic were presented at the International R.S. Prussia Convention in 1991. Lee Marple's (1991) presentation focused on the Hidden Image Mold which is sometimes found with the Saxe Altenburg mark. He also noted that RSP Mold 343 is a common mold found with the Saxe Altenburg mark. Colleen Norman and Rose Greider (1991) presented a study showing that a number of floral decorations found on unmarked china were the same as those found on china with the Saxe Altenburg mark. Slides of examples were shown for both studies. The connection between the Saxe Altenburg mark and some Schlegelmilch molds and decorations was apparent. But other Saxe Altenburg marked china was decorated with floral transfers which appear to be unique to the Saxe Altenburg mark. Consequently, unmarked china with a documented Saxe Altenburg decoration should be attributed to the Saxe Altenburg mark rather than to a Schlegelmilch mark (or factory).

A relatively small number of molds and decorations with the Saxe Altenburg mark match a marked Schlegelmilch mold or decoration. Some of the Altenburg marked molds which do match are the same ones which are also found with a Star mark. The most logical explanation for this overlapping of molds among Schlegelmilch marks, Star marks, and Saxe Altenburg marks is that one of the factories purchased blanks from another. The factories which used either the Star or the Saxe Altenburg marks could have purchased blanks from the Schlegelmilchs, or vice versa — the Schlegelmilchs could have purchased blanks from some other factory. It is impossible to know what occurred. The practice of one factory purchasing blanks from another factory, however, was common among European china manufacturers. A factory might purchase blanks to decorate before its own production was fully underway. Factories also purchased blanks from other potteries when their own orders exceeded their production, and they were not able to make enough china to fill those orders.

Floral transfer designs which appear to be unique to the Saxe Altenburg mark are identified with the word "Saxe" and lower case letters "a" through "d." Unmarked examples which have one of these Saxe decorations are shown after the Saxe marked pieces. Some of the unmarked items with Saxe decorations may also represent a Steeple mold, and that is noted in the caption for the photograph. In Norman and Greider's presentation (1991), it was suggested that the gold tracery or stencilled designs which make up a large part of the border decorations on many pieces might be used to differentiate unmarked china as being either connected to the Saxe Altenburg mark or to a Schlegelmilch mark.

All china featured in this section, with one exception, either has a Saxe Altenburg mark or is unmarked. One piece has an embossed Star mark. It is decorated with a Saxe pattern, however. The Star marked object has been placed here to demonstrate an example of a connection between Star marked china and Saxe Altenburg marked china.

Saxe Altenburg Mark 1, "Germany Saxe Altenburg" in red.

Saxe Altenburg Mark 2, "Germany (Crown) Saxe Altenburg."

Plate 489. *Bowl, 9"d, Mold is the same as bowl in Plate 483 under Embossed Star marks; Saxe Floral Decoration (Saxe FDa), a spray of pink and white lilies; gold stencilled designs in three places around border extending toward center; light pink and yellow finish around outer border; Saxe Altenburg Mark 1.*

Plate 490. *Oval Bowl, 13¼"l x 9¼"w, elaborate pierced work around border highlights this floral mold; Saxe FDa; tinted blue border; Saxe Altenburg Mark 1.*

Plate 492. *Bowl, 10½"d, Steeple Mold 3; Saxe FDc, yellow roses with mixed flowers; rose finish on outer border; gold stencilled designs; Saxe Altenburg Mark 1.*

Plate 491. *Chocolate Pot, Steeple Mold 12; Saxe FDb, clusters of small orange and white flowers; purple finish with white shadow flowers on alternate panels around top and on base; Saxe Altenburg Mark 1.*

Plate 494. *Bowl, RSP Mold 343 (Steeple Mold 8); Saxe FDd; Steeple BG3; Saxe Altenburg Mark 1.*

Plate 493. *Cake Plate, 11½"d, RSP Mold 343 (Steeple Mold 8); Saxe FDd, white and yellow jonquils outlined in gold; Steeple BG3, overall cobalt blue finish; gold stencilled designs and scroll work; Saxe Altenburg Mark 1.*

Plate 495. *Chocolate Cup, 3¼"h, companion to RSP Mold 343 (Steeple Mold 8) with rim variation; Steeple FDQ, pink, yellow, and white mums; dark green finish on borders; gold stencilled designs; Saxe Altenburg Mark 2.*

Plate 496. *Plate, 7¾"d, RSP Mold 343 (Steeple Mold 8); Steeple FDR, large yellow flower with smaller multicolored flowers; figural reserves around border (girl on swing); iridescent Tiffany border overlaid with gold stencilled designs; Saxe Altenburg Mark 1.*

Plate 497. *Ewer, 11"h, an RSG Mold; Diana The Huntress figural cameo; iridescent Tiffany finish; Cherub decor opposite handle (not shown); Saxe Altenburg Mark 1.*

Plate 498. *Shaving Mug, 3½"h; Saxe FDa, pink and white lilies; Tiffany iridescent finish on border; unmarked.*

164

Plate 499. Bowl, 10"d; Saxe FDa; gold stencilled inner border; green and brown finish around outer border; unmarked.

Plate 500. Plate, 8¾"d; detailed molded designs on body of plate; Saxe FDa, pink and white lilies; light blue finish; unmarked.

Plate 501. Plate, 6¾"d; Saxe FDa; gold stencilled designs scattered around plate; blue tinted finish; unmarked.

Plate 502. Relish Dish, 9½"l x 4"w, RSP Mold 343 (Steeple Mold 8); Saxe FDa with Steeple FDI around outer border; gold stencilled designs scattered around interior of dish; light blue inner border; unmarked.

Plate 503. Plate, 7⅝"d, RSP Mold 343 (Steeple Mold 8); Saxe FDb, small orange and white flowers in center with Star FDc, pink and yellow roses, alternating with Saxe FDc around outer border; cobalt blue inner border with gold stencilled designs; unmarked.

Plate 505. *Oval Bowl, 12½"l, a floral mold similar to Steeple Mold 6 (Iris Variation Mold); Saxe FDd, white and yellow jonquils outlined in gold; Steeple BG3, overall cobalt blue finish; gold highlights; unmarked.*

Plate 504. *Cake Plate, 10½"d; Saxe FDa; gold stencilled inner border; green finish with white flowers and shadow flowers around outer border; unmarked.*

Plate 507. *Cracker Jar, 7½"h, companion to RSP Mold 343 (steeple Mold 8); Saxe FDd, white and yellow jonquils outlined in gold; Steeple BG3, overall cobalt blue finish; gold beaded edge; embossed star mark.*

Plate 506. *Pitcher, 8½"h, companion to RSP Mold 343 (Steeple Mold 8 with handle variation); Saxe FDd; Steeple BG3; gold highlights; unmarked.*

Plate 508. *Bowl, 10¾"d, free form mold as in Plate 480 (under Embossed Star Marks); Saxe FDd; Steeple BG3; unmarked.*

Plate 509. *Plate, 9"d, RSP Mold 343 (Steeple Mold 8); Saxe FDd, Steeple BG3; unmarked.*

167

Royal Vienna

Mark 15 in my first book illustrated the RSP mark with another mark, "Royal Vienna." I said (p. 25) that the Royal Vienna mark might mean that the pieces were made by the Schlegelmilch factory and then decorated by a studio using the Royal Vienna mark. The mark is always overglaze, in red, black, or gold. "Germany" may or may not be printed beneath the crown. The Royal Vienna mark can be found as a double mark with the RS Germany mark as well as the RSP mark.

Research about the Royal Vienna mark has not brought forth any facts about its origin. Hayden (1970: 12) said that the mark was a Schlegelmilch mark. That cannot be substantiated. Because the Royal Vienna mark is sometimes found with an RS mark, or even found alone on an RS mold, does not mean that the Royal Vienna mark was used by one of the Schlegelmilch factories. Like the Star marks and the Saxe Altenburg mark, the Royal Vienna mark appears to have some sort of link to Schlegelmilch china. What that link is remains unknown. The Art Nouveau shape, however, of many of the molds is compatible with a time period of the early 1900s, prior to World War I.

Although the RV mark is sometimes found as a double mark with other RS marks, the mark is more often found alone. The mark is also usually found on molds which cannot be identified as Schlegelmilch molds. The similarity of decoration transfers, however, between RV and RS marked china is seen more frequently. The basic differences between the two are that the Royal Vienna pieces are usually more elaborately shaped and more richly decorated. While the same portrait or figural transfers are found on RSP, the backgrounds are not as rich.

By studying the portrait and figural decorations commonly associated with R.S. Prussia china, it is apparent that many of those decorations are often on unmarked china. Collectors have considered the pieces as "Prussia" regardless of whether or not they had an RSP mark, or whether or not they matched a marked RSP mold. "Flora," "Diana the Huntress," "Madame Récamier," and "Countess Potocka" are just a few examples.

When comparing china with any of the RS marks, it seems that the Steeple marked items have more in common with Royal Vienna marked china. The Tiffany bronze finish which often accompanies the "Colonial Ladies" decor as well as the deep cobalt blue borders and finishes are most often found on Steeple marked china or unmarked pieces. These finishes are found on Royal Vienna marked examples as well. Some of the Steeple molds also resemble Royal Vienna molds. The Iris Variation mold (Steeple Mold 6) is an Art Nouveau shape as are many Royal Vienna molds.

The majority of pieces shown in this section have only the Royal Vienna mark. With the exception of a few objects, the molds are unique to the Royal Vienna mark rather than to any RS mark. I have numbered the molds (RV#) so that collectors can make an easy distinction between them and RSP molds. Where the same molds are found with an RSP or Steeple mark, the RSP or Steeple mold number has been used. One example (Plate 534) happens to be the same mold as a Saxe Altenburg marked piece shown in the previous section (Plate 497). This item is an Ewer which has also been found with an R.S. Germany mark as well. Such pieces point out the overlap between Schlegelmilch china and china with Ambiguous marks.

Note that RSP Molds 926 and 927 in G2 (p. 143) probably should be classified in general as Royal Vienna molds. One vase was unmarked, and the other had the Royal Vienna mark with an RSP mark. The elaborate shape of the mold as well as the richness of the background decoration is more characteristic of the Royal Vienna mark alone. This will be apparent in the photographs. Old RSP Mold 585 has been deleted from the RSP molds and moved to the Royal Vienna molds. Examples shown previously were unmarked, but Royal Vienna marked pieces have been found.

The decorations on the RV marked pieces are almost all figural or portrait. A few of the floral designs, however, are a Steeple decoration. The Steeple Decoration letter is shown in the captions for those pieces.

A few unmarked items are shown at the end of this section. These seem to fit the Royal Vienna image. The molds have not been documented to any RS marked mold. Thus, it seems reasonable to attribute them to the Royal Vienna mark, especially when the decoration and finish on the unmarked pieces are the same as those found on a Royal Vienna marked example.

Royal Vienna Mark 1 in gold, red, or black.

Royal Vienna Mark 2 with "Germany" in red, gold, or black.

Plate 510. *Vase, 13"h, Royal Vienna (RV) Mold 1; Lady with Fan decor; cobalt blue finish overlaid with gold stencilled flowers; RV Mark 1.*

Plate 511. *Vase, 13"h, RV Mold 1; Lady Feeding Chickens figural decor; cobalt blue finish with gold stencilled floral design; RV Mark 1.*

Plate 512. Vase, 8¾"h, RV Mold 1; Countess Litta portrait; lavender finish with yellow highlights; RV Mark 2 in red.

Plate 514. Vases: Left, 9"h; Right, 4½"h (salesman's sample); RV Mold 1; Steeple FDU, yellow and pink roses; cobalt blue finish; unmarked.

Plate 513. Vase, 9"h, RV Mold 1; Lady Seated with Dog figural scene; multicolored finish; gold trim; unmarked.

170

Plate 516. *Vase, 7½"h, RV Mold 2; Lady Feeding Chickens figural scene; bronze Tiffany iridescent finish; gold trim; RV Mark 1.*

Plate 515. *Vase, 9¼"h, RV Mold 2; Madame LeBrun II portrait; gold frame with beaded work; green and lavender tinted background; Greek Key design in gold around center; gold stencilled floral designs; RV Mark 1 in gold.*

Plate 517. *Ewer, 8"h, RV Mold 3; Peasant Girl portrait; lavender finish with yellow highlights; RV Mark 2.*

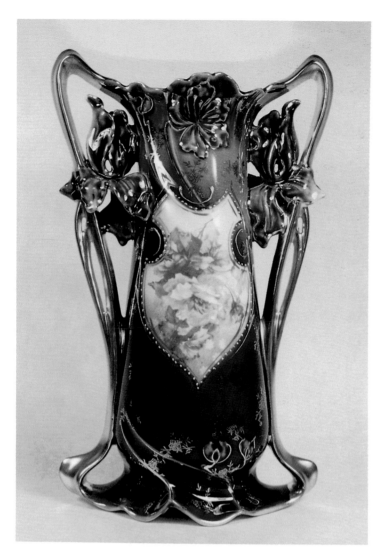

Plate 518. Vase, 9⅜"h, RV Mold 4, large molded iris on sides of vase; Steeple FDU, yellow-gold and pink roses; cobalt blue finish; gold stencilled designs and gold trim; RV Mark 2 in red.

Plate 519. Vase, 9"h, RV Mold 4; Lady with Fan figural decor; Tiffany iridescent finish with gold stencilled designs; unmarked.

Plate 520. Reverse of Vase in Plate 519; Lady Feeding Chickens.

Plate 521. *Tankard, 11¾"h, RV Mold 5, molded flower at top of handle; "Flossie" portrait; cobalt blue finish; gold trim; RV Mark 2 in red.*

Plate 522. *Tankard, 11¾"h, RV Mold 5; Steeple FDI, lavender to yellow tinted poppies; RV Mark 2 in red.*

Plate 523. *Vase, 9"h, RV Mold 6; unidentified woman's portrait; cobalt blue background; RV Mark 2 in red.*

Plate 524. Vase, 8½"h, RV Mold 7; Diana The Huntress scene on front; (Flora on reverse); iridescent finish; RV Mark 2.

Plate 525. Vase, 9¾"h, RV Mold 8; Diana The Huntress on front (Flora on reverse and Cherubs to the right and left of portraits); cobalt blue finish with gold stencilled floral designs; RV Mark 2 in red.

Plate 526. Oval Bowl, 11½" x 6⅛", footed, RV Mold 9; Flora figural scene on front with Diana The Huntress on reverse; Cherubs between portraits; iridescent Tiffany finish; RV Mark 2.

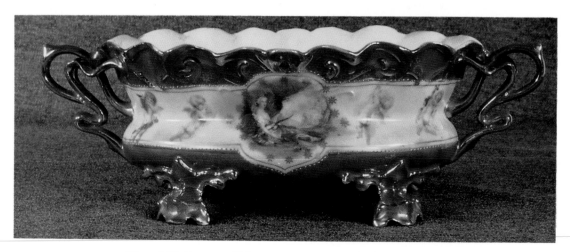

Plate 527. Reverse of Plate 526 showing Diana The Huntress.

174

Plate 528. *Vase, 11"h, RV Mold 10; Countess Potocka portrait; lavender finish on top border and around middle of vase; gold Greek Key design; gold trim; RV Mark 2.*

Plate 529. *Vase, 7¼"h, RV Mold 11; LeBrun I portrait; green luster background; gold stencilled designs; RV Mark 2.*

Plate 530. *Vase, 11¾"h, RV Mold 11; Diana The Huntress; iridescent finish overlaid with gold stencilled floral designs; RV Mark 2.*

Plate 531. *Reverse of Vase in Plate 530 with Flora (or Reclining Lady) portrait.*

175

Plate 532. *Vase, 8¾"h, RV Mold 12; Steeple FDB, multicolored mums; green and yellow background; gold trim; RV Mark 2 in red.*

Plate 533. *Vase, 11"h, RV Mold 13; Madame Récamier portrait; cobalt blue finish on top border, base, and around portrait; gold beaded frame work; gold stencilled designs; RV Mark 2.*

Plate 534. *Ewer, 11"h, RSG Mold; Semi-Nude Woman Bathing at Well; cobalt blue finish; gold trim; RV Mark 2.*

Plate 535. *Vase, 7"h, RV Mold 14; LeBrun II portrait; shaded green background; RV Mark 2 in gold.*

Plate 536. *Vase, 5½"h, RV Mold 15; Steeple FDX, pink roses with a watered silk finish; RV Mark 2 in gold.*

Plate 537. *Vase, 6½"h, R.S. Steeple Mold 12; Flora figural decor on front and Diana The Huntress on reverse (not shown); lavender iridescent finish; RV Mark 2.*

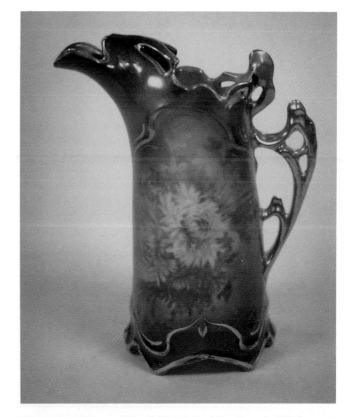

Plate 538. *Ewer, 5"h, RSP Mold 640; Steeple FDQ, pink, yellow, and white mums on light to dark green background; gold trim; RV Mark 2.*

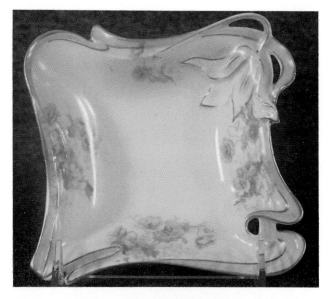

Plate 539. *Bowl, 5⅛"sq., RSP Mold 40; small pink floral design around outer border; tinted light green finish; gold trim; RV Mark 1 in gold.*

Plate 540. *Covered Sugar Bowl, 4½"h, RSP Mold 576; small roses around upper border; RV Mark 1 in gold.*

Plate 541. *Vase, 5½"h; Diana The Huntress decorates front and Flora is on reverse (not shown); iridescent Tiffany finish; gold stencilled floral designs; unmarked (decor and finish are typical of Royal Vienna marked china).*

Plate 543. *Vase, 7"h, same mold as Vase in Plate 542; Madame Récamier portrait; lavender iridescent finish; unmarked.*

Plate 542. *Vase, 9½"h; Diana The Huntress (front) with Flora (back, not shown); cobalt blue finish with gold stencilled floral designs; unmarked.*

178

Other Royal and Red Crown Marks

A few Schlegelmilch molds and decorations as well as some Royal Vienna molds can be found with other marks which have the word "Royal" as part of the mark. These marks are not double marked with any RS mark. A few examples are shown. The Royal Berlin Mark is shown on RSP Molds 347 and 657 (companion molds). Some unmarked pieces with the same, or similar, decorations are included under this mark.

The Royal Coburg mark is shown on a Royal Vienna mold as well as on RSP Mold 343 (Steeple Mold 8). The Royal Erfurt mark is on RSP Mold 29. The Royal Frankfort mark is on Royal Vienna Mold 6 and RSP Mold 517. The decorations on these pieces span various marks with the floral transfers identified as Steeple designs. The portrait and figural themes are those found on RSP, Steeple, and Royal Vienna china.

Two examples of marks with the words "Royal Tillowitz" are included here as ambiguous marks. The marks do not incorporate the RS initials. The first mark is on a demi-tasse cup. It is in conjunction with an embossed star shaped mark (unlike the Star marks in the preceding section). The second mark is on RSP mold 256. Another collector sent a photo of a mark similar to the latter, except "Oldenburg" rather than "Tillowitz" is printed with that mark.

A red "Crown" mark is shown which seems to be almost the same, if not identical, to the Royal Vienna red crown. The mark is shown for RSP Molds 517, 614, 98, and 25a. The mark is also on the sugar bowl in Plate 560. That particular mold has not been identified with any Schlegelmilch mark. The decorations on these pieces are ones which are found on RSP or Steeple china.

The red crown in the "Viersa" mark is also like the one in the Royal Vienna mark and the single red crown mark described above. The Viersa mark, however, is usually found on pieces which have RS Germany shapes and floral patterns. It is sometimes seen as a double mark with the R.S. Germany mark. Thus another connection between Schlegelmilch marked china and these other ambiguous marks is noted.

*Royal Berlin Mark with a
Star in gold.*

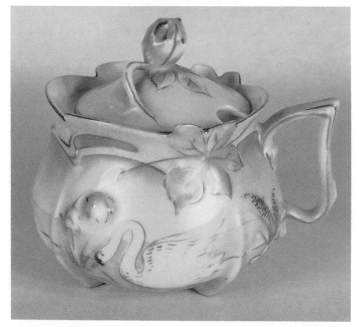

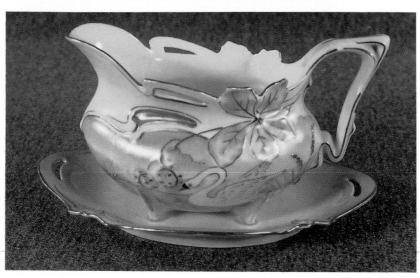

Plate 544. Plate, 7¾"d, RSP Mold 347; Swan outlined in gold with white water lilies; tinted blue background; Royal Berlin Mark.

Plate 545. Cracker Jar, 7¾"h, RSP Mold 657 (companion to RSP Mold 347); Swan decor (neck is different from one in Plate 544); gold cattails; blue background; satin finish; Royal Berlin Mark.

Plate 546. Mustard Jar, RSP Mold 657; Swan decor similar to decoration in Plate 544; satin finish; unmarked.

Plate 547. Gravy Boat and Underplate, RSP Mold 347; Swan decor; satin finish; unmarked.

Royal Coburg Mark with Crown shape and Germany in red.

Plate 548. *Vase, 10½"h, Royal Vienna Mold 1; "Flossie" portrait; lavender finish with yellow highlights; Royal Coburg Mark.*

Plate 549. *Mustard Pot, 3"h, companion to RSP Mold 343 (Steeple Mold 8); Steeple FDQ, pink, yellow, and white mums; dark green finish; Royal Coburg Mark.*

Plate 550. *Tea Set: Creamer, Teapot, Covered Sugar Bowl, companion to RSP Mold 343 (Steeple Mold 8); Lady Feeding Chickens on creamer; Lady with Fan on teapot; Lady Watering Flowers on sugar bowl; Steeple BG2, cobalt blue border with white flowers; Royal Coburg Mark with Star Mark 1 and raised bar marks (similar to old Marks 3 and 12 in G1 and G2).*

Royal Erfurt Mark
with Germany in red.

Royal Frankfort Mark
with Germany in red.

Plate 551. *Bowl, 6½"d, RSP Mold 29 (variation); Steeple FDS, large yellow roses; Royal Erfurt Mark.*

Plate 552. *Cup, 2⅛"h, RSP Mold 517 (Lily Mold, companion to RSP Mold 29); a pink and yellow rose; Royal Frankfort Mark.*

Plate 553. *Vase, 11¾"h, Royal Vienna Mold 2; Castle scene on green to yellow background; gold trim; Royal Frankfort Mark.*

Plate 554. *Cake Plate, 9¾"d, R.S. Steeple Mold 6 (Iris Variation Mold); gold stencilled floral designs on white body; Royal Hamburg Germany mark. (Mark not shown but is the same style as the Royal Frankfort mark.)*

Royal Oldenburg Mark in red. Example of item not shown. Style of Mark is the same as in following Royal Tillowitz mark.

Royal Tillowitz Mark 1 in red.

Plate 555. *Plate, 6"d, RSP Mold 256; double pink roses; Tiffany iridescent finish on sections separating scallops; Royal Tillowitz Mark 1.*

Royal Tillowitz Mark 2 in red, variation of Royal Tillowitz Mark 1.

Plate 556. *Demi-tasse Cup, 2"h, and Saucer; small lavender and yellow flowers around inner border; gold enameled inner border; lavender finish; Royal Tillowitz Mark 2.*

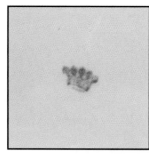

Red Crown Mark (similar to crown in Royal Vienna and Viersa Marks).

Plate 557. Bowl, 7¼"l, RSP Mold 25b, Iris Variation Mold; Mill scene; cobalt blue border; Red Crown Mark.

Plate 558. Chocolate Pot, RSP Mold 517 (Companion to RSP Mold 29); Steeple FDS, large yellow roses; Red Crown Mark.

Plate 559. Covered Sugar Bowl and Creamer, RSP Mold 614; small white and pink roses; Red Crown Mark.

184

Plate 560. *Covered Sugar Bowl, 4¾"h; same rose transfer as in Plate 559; Red Crown Mark.*

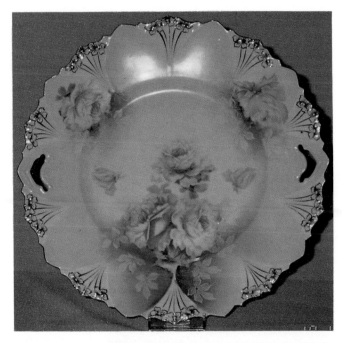

Plate 561. *Cake Plate, 11¼"d, RSP Mold 98; RSP FD5a, two pink roses; Red Crown Mark.*

Viersa with Red Crown Mark.

Plate 562. *Bowl, 10"d, companion to RSP Mold 343 (Steeple Mold 8); Steeple FDS, large yellow roses; cobalt blue border with gold stencilled designs; Viersa Mark.*

185

Other Ambiguous Marks

Several other ambiguous marks which appear to have something in common with Schlegelmilch china conclude this section. An "R.S. Celebrate, Germany" mark could be attributed to the RS factory. The mold of the pieces with the mark are shaped in forms more similar to Steeple marked china than to china with other RS marks.

An "RS" mark without "Germany" is distinguished by an arrow separating the initials. Some lettering below the initials is too blurred to decipher. The mark is on a butter dish decorated with a tapestry type finish. This is similar to the finish found on some of the production of the E.S. Factory (see G2, Plate 439).

Another mark which is on an R.S. Germany mold is "Regina Ware." The decoration is a stylized floral pattern like those used on R.S. Germany china. Röntgen (1980: 94) shows a similar mark. It is noted as unidentified.

R.S. Celebrate and Crown Mark in red or green.

Plate 563. *Open Sugar Bowl, 1½"h, and Creamer, 2½"h (demi-tasse or child's toy china size); floral decor appears to be handpainted; RS Celebrate Mark.*

R.S. and Arrow Mark in black.

Plate 564. *Covered Butter Dish (with drainer not shown), 3½"h x 7"d; tapestry type finish in pink and white with stylized floral designs and black outlining; RS Arrow Mark.*

*Regina Ware and
Crown Mark in green.*

Plate 565. *Covered Sugar Bowl, 3¾"h, R.S. Germany mold and floral decor, white lilies; Regina Ware Mark.*

Children's China and Novelties

Children's china or toy dishes and a few other novelties or unique objects are featured in this section. Such pieces are rarely found with marks. Sometimes "Germany" may be stamped or impressed on the bases of the items, but no factory is identified. Some examples of this type of china are often considered as "Prussia" by collectors because the decorations are the same as those found on marked Schlegelmilch china. The molds may also be the same or similar. Children's china is listed as part of the production of the R.S. Schlegelmilch factories in the Ceramic Directories published while the factories were in operation.

The china shown in this section is all unmarked. Some of the pieces do have typical decorations associated with RS marks such as the Farm and Lake scenes, Lions, Countess Potocka, and Countess Litta. One piece, however, has a floral transfer which is found on Star marked china (see the preceding section on Ambiguous Marks).

The mold of the vertical pieces in the tea set decorated with the Farm scene is similar to some RSP molds as is the fruit decorated set. The two cup and saucer sets are RSP Mold 627a. The bells are shown side by side with RSP marked cups. The pictures illustrate how both pieces are decorated with the same floral designs.

Plate 566. *Child's Toy Dinner Service: Teapot, 5"h; Covered Sugar Bowl, 3"h; Creamer, 3"h; 2 Serving Plates, 4¾"d; 4 Plates, 3¾"d; 4 Cups, 1½"h; and Saucers, 3⅜"d; Embossed Star FDa, small multicolored flowers; blue border; gold trim; unmarked.*

Plate 567. *Child's Toy Tea Set: Covered Sugar Bowl, Teapot, Creamer, 2 Cake Plates, 4 Cups and Saucers; Farm and House by Lake scenic decor; gold trim; unmarked.*

Plate 568. *Child's Toy Tea Set: Covered Sugar Bowl, 4¼"h; Cup, 2¼"h, and Saucer (6 in set); Teapot, 6½"h; Creamer, 3½"h; Lion and Tiger transfers; pink border; luster finish; unmarked.*

Plate 569. *Child's Toy Tea Set: Cup, 1⅛"h; Saucer, 2¼"d; Covered Sugar Bowl, 2"h; Teapot, 3"h; Creamer, 1⅞"h; Countess Potocka decorates Teapot; floral reserves on Creamer and Sugar Bowl; cobalt blue finish with gold stencilled designs; unmarked.*

Plate 570. *Child's Toy Tea Set (for 6): Covered Sugar Bowl, 3"h; Cup, 2½"h, and Saucer; Teapot, 5¼"h; Creamer, 2¼"h; RSP Fruit I (mixed fruit) and Fruit V (pears and grapes) decor; gold trim; unmarked.*

Plate 571. *Child's Toy Tea Set: Creamer, Covered Sugar Bowl, Teapot, Cups, and Saucers; roses on blue tinted background; center medallions outlined in gold; unmarked.*

Plate 573. *Child's doll size Tea Cups (set of 6): Cups, 1⅛"h; Saucers, 2⅝"d; RSP Mold 627a; green finish on alternating sections around top; gold trim; unmarked.*

Plate 572. *Child's Tea Cup, 2"h, and Saucer, 3⅞"d, RSP Mold 627a; cobalt blue finish shading to white; gold trim; unmarked.*

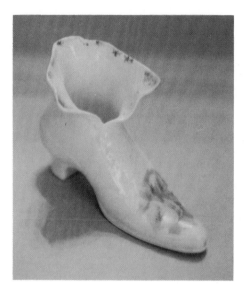

Plate 574. *Child's doll size mug, 1½"h; Countess Litta portrait; scrolled gold designs form frame; light green finish; unmarked.*

Plate 575. *Novelty Shoe, 3"h, 4"l; pink roses; unmarked.*

Plate 576. *Bell, 4¼"h (with wooden clapper); red berry and green leaf decor; unmarked. (Decoration matches cup which has RSP Mark 1.)*

Plate 577. *Bell, 4¼"h (with wooden clapper on wire hanger); small pink roses and daisies; unmarked. (Decoration is the same as the demi-tasse cup which has RSP Mark 1.)*

Fake R.S. Marks and Reproductions

Some examples of the faked R.S. Prussia mark and misleading "R.S." marks which were shown in my earlier books are reprinted here. Some other new versions of the fake decal RSP mark are also included as well as a new R.S. Suhl fake mark. While the fake RSP wreath marks have looked relatively authentic, the fake RS Suhl mark does not. It is too large, and the letter "l" in Suhl is capitalized (L). That letter in the authentic mark is in the lower case.

Antique malls, shops, and flea markets carry many of these new items. The same lines of pieces and patterns which were being made in the early 1980s are still being made. Sometimes the marks on the pieces are the fake RSP mark or the misleading R.S. Wreath marks. But many of those items now have the fake R.S. Suhl mark. The same pieces can also be found with fake Limoges and Nippon marks. There is also another mark appearing on similar items. This mark is sometimes referred to as "Crown Prussia." It consists of a crown with a "P" beneath the crown.

While all of the contemporary china is certainly not equal in quality to Schlegelmilch china, collectors and dealers continue to be "taken" by these modern pieces. Usually the price can be the clue to whether or not the item is genuine. Beware of low prices. When these pieces are offered for sale in most retail outlets, the prices are not exorbitant, but they are still somewhat higher than what the importer sells them for. The bell shown in the following photographs was priced at $6.00 at one outlet, while down the road, another was selling it for $14.00.

Higher prices on these reproductions are often found at antique shows. Chocolate sets like those shown here have been seen with price tags of $200.00. A fair price for such modern pieces would be less than $40.00.

The importers continue to place gold stick-on labels on the pieces. These stickers may carry the name of the importer as well as the notation of "Made in Japan." Collectors who purchase these items with the stickers still on them really have no one but themselves to blame for buying such reproductions. The stickers, of course, are easily removed, and thus unscrupulous dealers simply take them off and price according to "what the market will bear." (Isn't it amazing how easily these stickers can be removed. Most stickers on their modern goods are glued on so well that one must scrub them off or even resort to using some form of chemical remover!)

The reproductions which were shown in the *First Series* have been reprinted here. While some of these are still being made, new patterns have also been introduced. Examples of four of the new designs are shown along with one picture of the pattern which has the "Crown Prussia" mark. No prices are listed in the Price Guide for these reproductions. Dealers should purchase catalogs from wholesale houses to keep abreast of new items and patterns of modern reproductions. Collectors should routinely be alert to large displays of china offered for sale which have floral, figural, or portrait decorations with RSP or RS Suhl marks. Examine marks and china carefully and ask the dealer for a money back guarantee if the item turns out to be a modern reproduction.

Repaired porcelain may cause almost as much concern for collectors as the fake marks and modern reproductions. I discussed this topic in the first edition. Businesses have been specializing in repairing R.S. Prussia for many years. It is inevitable that such pieces eventually find their way on the market. Some collectors desire to have a piece repaired when it becomes damaged. There is nothing wrong with that. The problem, of course, occurs when such pieces are later sold without the buyer being aware that a repair has been made.

There is certainly no rule of thumb for knowing whether or not a piece of china has been repaired. Professional china restorers are quite skillful. Some are less adept than others, however. Pieces may "fall apart," or handles, feet, and finials may come off pieces which have been improperly or hastily repaired. Collectors should always examine china carefully in a good, natural light. The eyes can deceive, and thus the object should be examined by going over the surface by hand as well. See that lids really fit and that all handles and feet match. Check for roughness or unevenness of body texture. Again, the best advice is to purchase from reputable dealers who stand behind their merchandise.

Repaired china should not be priced the same as china in good condition. R.S. Prussia prices, however, are often quite similar for repaired pieces and those in good condition. This is not likely to change until collectors begin to demand that not only are repairs indicated by sellers, but also that repaired pieces' prices are proportionately discounted according to the amount of damage.

Fake R.S. Prussia Mark 1.

Fake R.S. Prussia Mark 2.

Fake R.S. Prussia Mark 3.

Fake R.S. Mark 4, red wreath and star with initials.

Fake R.S. Prussia Mark 5, red wreath and star with initials.

Misleading Wreath Mark in green, Mark 6.

R1. Jewel Box, 10"l, 8"w; "signed" Boucher, Fake Mark 1, 5, or Fake R.S. Suhl mark. Similar boxes with other designs are also made.

R2. Egg Box, 5½"l; "signed" Boucher; Misleading Wreath Mark 6.

R3. Plate, 7"d; "signed" Boucher; Fake Mark 4.

R4. Bell, 5¼"h; same pastoral scene as preceding three photos. This example does not have a "signature"; Fake Mark 4.

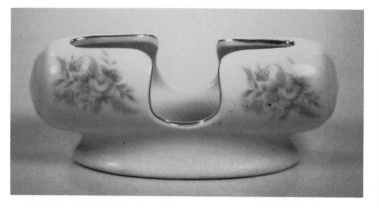

R5. Card Holder, 4½"l; pink rose pattern; Fake mark 3.

R6. Pitcher, 12"h; roses with cobalt blue finish; Fake Mark 2.

R7. Cracker Jar, 8"h; yellow rose pattern; Fake Mark 5.

R9. Hatpin Holder, 5½"h; pink rose pattern on light blue background; Fake Mark 4.

R8. Left-Handed Mustache Cup, 3" x 3¾", and Saucer, 7"d; yellow rose pattern; Fake Mark 5.

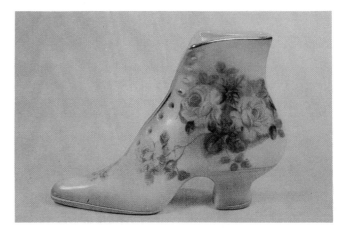

R11. Shoe with high top; pink rose pattern; Fake Mark 4.

R12. Saucer, 5½"d; pink rose pattern; Fake Mark 4.

R10. Ewer, 5"h (like RSP Mold 640); pink rose pattern on light blue and pink background; Fake Mark 4.

R13. Candy Dish, 8"l x 6"w (like RSP Mold 528 in G1, Plate 353); multicolored roses; Misleading Wreath Mark 6.

197

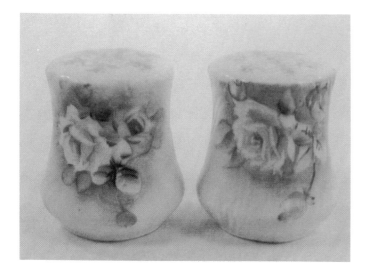

R14. Salt and Pepper Shakers, 2½"h; pink roses; Fake Mark 2.

R15. Mustache Cup, 3½"h; pink roses, wide gold border; Fake Mark 2.

R16. Cracker Jar, 7"h; pink rose spray, gold trim; Fake Mark 2.

R17. Cracker Jar, 5"h, no handles; pink roses; Fake Mark 2.

R18. *Bowl, 16"d; Pitcher, 11½"h; transfer portrait of Countess Potocka with "Monreau" as signature on lower right side of bust. This is not an RSP transfer. Pieces have Fake Mark 1.*

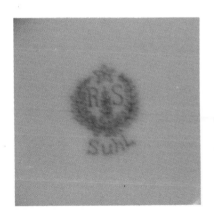

Fake R.S. Suhl Mark, spelled "SuhL."

R19. *Coffee Set: Pot, Covered Sugar Bowl, Creamer, and Cup and Saucer; pink rose pattern on tinted blue and pink background; Fake R.S. Suhl Mark.*

R20. *Chocolate Set: Pot and Mugs; light pink poppies in a stylized design; Fake R.S. Suhl Mark.*

R21. *Footed Bowl, 13"l, 6⅛"h, pierced work around border; cluster of pink roses with beige tinted borders and gold trim; Fake R.S. Suhl Mark.*

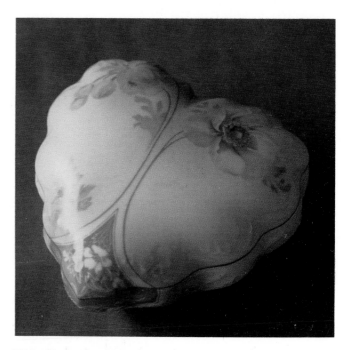

R22. *Heart-shaped Box, 5" x 5"; light pink poppies in a stylized design; Fake R.S. Suhl Mark.*

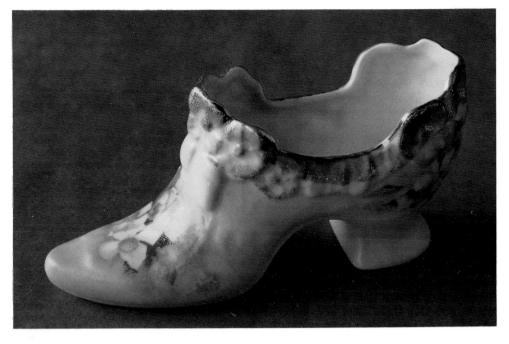

R23. *Shoe, 6½"l; two white dogwood blossoms with a pink flower; blue border with gold spattered work; Fake R.S. Suhl Mark.*

R24. *Muffineer, 4½"h; pale pink and lavender roses; Fake R.S. Suhl Mark.*

Misleading Crown and "P" Mark (described as "Crown Prussia" Mark).

R25. *Rectangular Box with pierced opening; Vase; Shell-shaped Dish; yellow rose pattern on tinted blue background; Misleading Crown and "P" Mark.*

Erdmann Schlegelmilch Marks and Photographs
Brown Marks
Green Crown Marks
Prov Sxe Marks
Beehive Marks
Other E.S. Marks
Ambiguous Marks, Molds, and Decorations

Comparison of Dating Information for ES Marks

Mark	Röntgen (1980)	Danckert (1984)	Zühlsdorff (1988)	Gaston (1986)
Cursive Brown Monogram	-----	-----	-----	circa 1880s
ES Bird in Oval/Ribbon with Suhl	1886 – 1938	-----	1927 – 1936	-----
ES Brown Bird in Oval	1896 – 1938	-----	1886 – 1910	1880s
ES Brown Bird with "Suhl" in Circle	1896 – 1938	-----	1886 – 1910	1880s
ES Green Bird in shield	– ca. 1938	-----	after 1910 – 1936	1920s – 1930s
Crown with "Royal Saxe"	after 1900	1902	after 1890 – 1910	1890s
Prov Sxe	after 1902 – 1938	1902	1902 – 1927	1900 – 1920
Beehive with Dot/Germany	after 1900 – 1938	-----	after 1910 – 1927	1900 – 1920
ES Green Monogram	after 1900 – 1938	-----	-----	1920s – 1930s

My suggested chronology for the ES marks presented in the *Second Series* remains basically the same for this edition. I have constructed a chart comparing Röntgen's, Danckert's, and Zühlsdorff's dates for those marks. My dating periods for the ES marks which appeared in the *Second Series* are also included.

From this chart one major discrepancy is found with one of the ES bird marks. The mark is composed of a bird in a dotted circle with a ribbon at the top. "E.S. Suhl" is printed in the mark. Röntgen indicates the mark was used from 1886, but Zühlsdorff lists the beginning year for the mark as 1927. I have not seen this particular mark on an example. The color of the mark as well as the decoration on china with the mark would help to determine whether the mark is one from the late 1880s or from the late 1920s.

I said in the *Second Series* that I thought the ES bird marks with the exception of old ES Mark 18, green bird in shield, were probably early ES marks. Röntgen shows the two other brown bird marks used from 1896. Zühlsdorff lists 1886 for one and 1896 for the other. Thus, the time of the 1880s to 1890s is probably the correct period.

I suggested the 1890s for the Royal Saxe with Crown marks, and I continue to support that date. That mark should pre-date the Prov Sxe marks, although the two could have overlapped. Röntgen, Danckert, and Zühlsdorff show 1901 as the first year for the mark. This reflects the time when the mark was first registered. Zühlsdorff indicates the mark was not used after 1927, while Röntgen simply shows the last date as his closing date for the factory, 1938. I said the mark was probably not used after the 1920s, and that seems to be a logical assumption.

Röntgen shows the Beehive with Dot mark to have been used between 1900 and 1938. Zühlsdorff lists the years of 1910 to 1936 for the mark. My time period for the mark was 1900 through the 1920s. We know that the mark overlapped with the Prov Sxe mark, because the beehive is part of one version of the Prov Sxe mark.

Zühldorff does not show the ES monogram mark, and Danckert does not list any dates for the mark. Röntgen shows the mark was used after 1900 until 1938. As I stated in the *Second Series*, that is too broad a time period, and the pieces with the mark appear to be later than 1900. They seem to reflect a time of the 1920s or 1930s.

A few ES marks are seldom, if ever, found on examples. "Suhl" printed inside a small oval shape with a wreath and bow at the top is one mark attributed to the ES Factory which to my knowledge has not been found by collectors in the United States. Kramer (1985) indicates that mark as well as the script mark of "E. Schlegelmilch/Germany" as the first marks used by the factory. Without examples of the "Suhl" wreath and bow mark, it is impossible to know if this is correct. The few examples found with the script mark, however, appear to be much later than the 1860s. Such pieces are shaped and decorated similarly to RS Germany and RS Tillowitz china made during the 1920s and 1930s.

A new ES mark is shown by Hartwich (1984). It is in the form of a crude cursive "E" and "S" joined at the base of the letters with a small vertical "squiggly" mark. The mark is similar to the brown ES cursive mark and may well be an early ES mark.

The major ES marks are shown in the following chart with my suggested chronology and dating periods. These are basically the same as printed in the *Second Series*. These marks and their variations along with a few other ES marks are shown in this section.

It is still impossible to know which mark was the first one used by the ES factory. While a lot of European china was not marked during the 1860s, marks were common by the 1870s, especially for china exported to the United States. The earliest date shown by the German references for any ES mark is 1886. Surely, marks were instituted before that date. The company was founded in 1861. Thus, that is a period of twenty-five years when no marks were recorded for the factory.

The Ceramic Registration Table shown by Danckert is for marks registered from 1875. It is probably the case that marks were not formally registered prior to that year. Nevertheless, there are still eleven years between 1875 and 1886 when there is no record of ES marks. It is also apparent from the Registration Table that factories did not register all of their marks. It they had, those dates would surely have been noted with the marks for which no dates are shown by Danckert.

Revised Chronology for Major ES Marks	
Cursive Brown Monogram Marks	circa late 1880s
ES Brown Bird Marks	circa 1880s to 1890s
Crown with "Royal Saxe"	circa 1890s to early 1900s
Prov Sxe Marks	circa early 1900s to 1920s
Beehive with Dot	circa early 1900s to 1920s
ES Green Bird in Shield	circa 1920s to 1930s
ES Green Monogram Mark	circa 1920s to 1930s
ES Script Marks	after 1920s to 1930s

Brown Marks

Several E.S. Marks are printed in brown. These include the E.S. cursive monogram marks and three brown "bird" marks. These particular marks may be the earliest ES marks. The decoration on the pieces shown here as well as in the *Second Series* is not the transfer type found on most ES china. The decoration appears to be either hand stencilled designs filled in with color or handpainted. On pieces with ES cursive marks, the decoration is not only simple, but might be considered rather crudely applied. The items with the brown bird marks, however, are more artistic in shape and decor. The suggested time period for these E.S. marks is the 1880s through the 1890s. Please refer to pages 146 and 147 in the *Second Series* for other examples with these rare marks.

ES Mark 1, brown cursive script initials in a circle.

ES Mark 2, brown cursive script initials in a circle (slight variation from Mark 1) with "Depon" (registered) and numbers written above mark.

ES Mark 3, brown cursive initials with a bird in an oval circle.

ES Mark 4, brown bird in a circle with "E." and "S." printed on either side of the circle and "Suhla" and "Germany" printed above and below the circle.

Plate 579. *Covered Bowl or Butter Dish, 4¾"h; white flowers and green leaves with a wide blue strip in a fish scale pattern across lid. ES Mark 1 with "Depon" and "3804."*

Plate 578. *Pitcher, water size; leaf decor on light green body with orange panels painted across body in a random design; ES Mark 1.*

Plate 581. *Cup, 2¾"h, and Saucer; white grapes on green and brown marbled background; light green interior with branches of leaves; gold rim; Saucer shades from dark to light green; ES Mark 2 on cup; Saucer is unmarked.*

Plate 580. *Covered Sugar Bowl, 3½"h; ribbed mold with applied handles; small pink flowers with autumn leaves; dark green finish on upper part of body; ES Mark 2.*

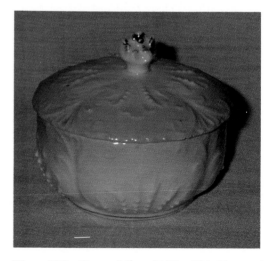

Plate 582. *Covered Jar, 3¼"h, 3"d; blue and white glossy finish; molded ribbed and beaded work on body; gold spattered work on finial; ES Mark 4.*

Green Crown Marks

The E.S. Crown mark is found with "Germany" printed below the crown and also with "Royal Saxe" printed above it. Another version of the mark has "1861" printed above the crown. The crown shape may have slight differences in design as shown in the several marks here. Pieces bearing these marks are often decorated with women's portraits. Indian themes usually have a Royal Saxe mark. Two examples with Oriental designs reflect the interest in the Far East which was prevalent during the 1890s and early 1900s. The floral decorated pieces are often on fancily shaped molds.

ES Mark 5, initials and Crown with Germany in green or blue-green.

ES Mark 6, initials and Crown with Germany and "Royal Saxe" above Crown in green.

ES Mark 7, similar to Mark 6 in green with numbers (for inventory) above mark.

ES Mark 8, similar to Mark 6 in blue.

ES Mark 9, Royal Saxe and Crown mark in green, slight variation in shape of Crown.

ES Mark 10, initials, Crown, and Germany with "1861" printed above Crown, in green; inventory numbers above mark.

Plate 584. Vase, 10"h, 3 handles; Mlle. Duboise portrait; green background with shadow flowers; gold handles and trim; ES Royal Saxe Mark.

Plate 583. Ewer, 12"h; Mademoiselle DuBoise portrait; gold frame with turquoise beaded work on pearl luster background; turquoise finish on neck and base highlighted by gold outlining and stencilled designs; gold handle; ES Mark 9.

Plate 585. Chocolate Pot; Mlle. DuBoise portrait with pearl luster and turquoise finish similar to Ewer in Plate 583; ES Mark 10.

Plate 586. *Vase, 2½"h, salesman's sample; woman's portrait; green finish with shadow flowers like Vase in Plate 584; gold bands with beaded work on neck and base; ES Mark 6.*

Plate 587. *Plate, 7"d, pointed scalloped border; Woman with Daisy Crown in hair; orange finish around outer border; ES Mark 10.*

Plate 588. *Plate, 7½"d; Victorian Woman's figural portrait; light blue flowers around outer border; gold highlights; ES Mark 9.*

Plate 589. *Plate, 7½"d; Victorian Woman's figural portrait with a back view; this decoration is in the same style as the figure in Plate 588; ES Mark 9.*

Plate 590. *Oval Bowl, 11⅞"l x 5⅞"w; portrait of a Woman with Holly Wreath in hair; gold frame around portrait; molded leaves and grapes around inner border extending into dish; ES Mark 9.*

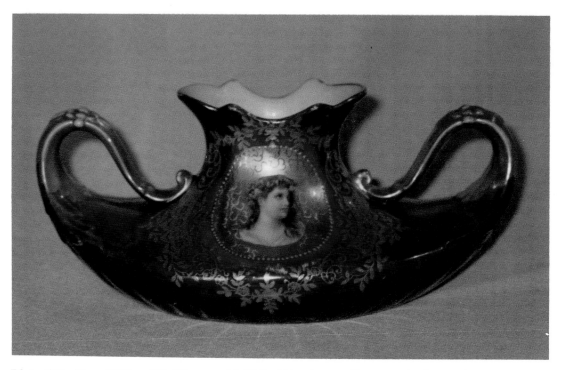

Plate 591. *Vase, 3½"h x 8"l; Woman with Holly Wreath on gold tapestry background; iridescent wine Tiffany finish overlaid with gold stencilled floral designs; ES Mark 5.*

Plate 592. *Bowl, 8⅜"d; Woman with Holly Wreath; pink outer border; gold stencilled floral designs; ES Mark 9.*

Plate 593. *One handled Dish, 7"d; Woman with Holly Wreath; gold beaded frame; dark green finish; gold stencilled designs; unmarked.*

Plate 594. *Bowl, two handles, 11½"d; Indian portrait decor, Chief High Hawk; turquoise border; gold trim; ES Mark 9.*

Plate 595. *Plate, 7"d; Indian portrait, Chief High Hawk; shaded green background with gold stencilled designs; ES Mark 9.*

Plate 596. Toothpick Holder, 2"h, hat shaped; Chief High Hawk portrait; ES Mark 9.

Plate 597. Child's toy china: Open Sugar Bowl, 2"h; Creamer, 2½"h; Indian decor, Chief Spotted Horse on Sugar Bowl; ES Mark 8.

Plate 598. Cracker Jar, 8"h; Chief Spotted Horse; gold stencilled designs form frame; peace pipe and staff design on sides; turquoise finish at top of jar; ES Royal Saxe Mark with "263/7574" (inventory numbers).

Plate 600. Vase, 6¼"h x 5"d; Oriental decor, gold birds with red highlights on dark cobalt blue background; white dragon shapes overlaid with gold designs; ES Mark 10.

Plate 599. Cracker Jar, 7"h; Indian portrait, Left Hand Bear; gold stencilled Indian symbols; tinted green finish; ES Mark 6.

Plate 601. Leaf Dish, 6"l x 4⅛"w; Underplate, 7⅛"l x 5¼"w; Oriental scenic decor with a woman's figure decorating interior of gravy or sauce dish; ES Mark 10 with mold number "164" impressed on base.

213

Plate 602. *Divided Dish, 5"l x 4"w, for eggs; an orange and a purple flower decorate recessed center; gold trim; ES Mark 8.*

Plate 603. *Desk Accessory: Letter Holder, 4¾"l; green with gold trim; ES Mark 7.*

Plate 604. *Bowl, 11"d; orange tinted azaleas with pink and yellow roses; gold trim; heavily scalloped mold with interior ribbed designs; ES Mark 10.*

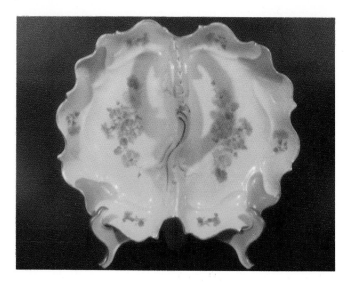

Plate 605. *Divided dish with center handle, 10½"l; pink and white flowers; pink finish in four places around outer border; ES Mark 9.*

Plate 606. *Candle Holder, 5⅞"h, square base, 2½"d; multicolored flowers scattered over surface; ES Mark 10 (without Germany).*

Plate 607. *Plate, 11½"d; azaleas decorate center with gold stencilled floral designs around outer border; green highlights around outer border; ES Mark 10.*

214

Prov Sxe Marks

The E.S. Prov Sxe marks are in green. They may or may not include "Germany." Prov Sxe mark 3 does not have the elliptical shape drawn around it as do the other versions of the mark. Mark 6 incorporates a Beehive with a dot. This particular style of Beehive mark is also found as a single mark on china. Most of the E.S. production found in this country has one of the Prov Sxe marks. The Art Nouveau shapes of the vases clearly identify the marks with the early 1900s. The vases and some table ware items are vividly decorated with portrait and figural themes, highlighted by richly colored borders. The figural transfers are based on classical, mythological, or allegorical subjects. Some other pieces are decorated with stylized floral designs, similar to those found on R.S. Germany china. Those examples are probably from a later period, circa the 1920s. Unmarked china which fits the Prov Sxe image is noted as being unmarked.

ES Mark 11, Prov Sxe with initials in ellipse, in green (with Crown and "N" in gold, special mark to denote Napoleon decor).

ES Mark 12, Prov Sxe with initials in ellipse, in green.

ES Mark 13, Prov Sxe with initials and German without ellipse, in green.

ES Mark 14, similar to Mark 13 with ellipse, in green.

ES Mark 15, Prov Sxe ellipse mark with Handpainted in script, in green.

ES Mark 16, Prov Sxe with initials and "Thuringia" in ellipse, in green.

ES Mark 17, Prov Sxe E.S. Germany mark with Beehive, in green.

Plate 608. Plate, 11¼"d, pierced work around four points on outer border; Lady with Swallows figural decor; bright pink poppies with enameled centers; dark cobalt blue outer border; gold accents; ES Mark 14.

Plate 609. Plate, 8½"d, same mold as shown in Plate 608; Goddess of Fire portrait; ES Mark 14.

Plate 610. *Cup and Saucer in same mold as Plates 608 and 609; Woman Holding Two Roses portrait; ES Mark 16.*

Plate 611. *Cracker Jar, 4½"h x 8½"w; Woman Holding One Rose; ES Mark 14.*

Plate 612. *Bowl, 10"d; woman's portrait; inner border decorated with wine and green panels overlaid with gold stencilled designs; ES Mark 14.*

Plate 613. *Plate, 8"d; Woman Holding Two Roses; gold stippled work on inner border; iridescent wine finish; ES Mark 13.*

217

Plate 614. Plate, 12"d; three figure mythological scene; floral reserves around outer border; wine finish; gold stencilled designs; ES Mark 14.

Plate 616. Plate, 8½"d; figural scene with a musical theme, two women and one man in Victorian dress; wine border with gold accents; ES Mark 14.

Plate 615. Plate, 8½"d; mythological scene with women and cherub; gold stencilled garlands around border; dark green finish with red accents and gold designs; ES Mark 14.

Plate 617. *Two handled Dish, 10"l x 5"w; figural scene of two women with a man holding flowers and a hat; wine finish with shadow flowers; ES Mark 16.*

Plate 618. *Cracker Jar; figural portrait of Woman Holding One Rose; turquoise finish with gold stencilled designs; ES Mark 13.*

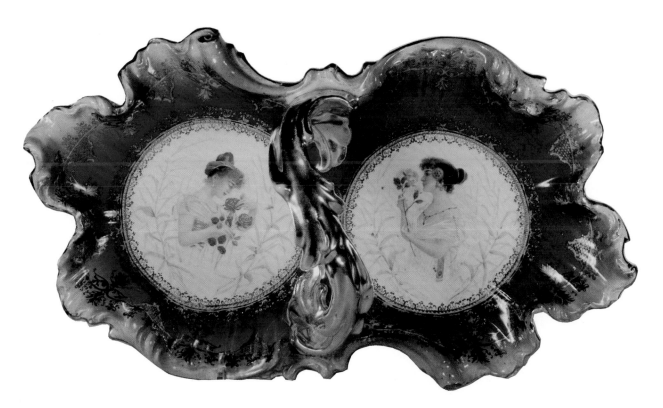

Plate 619. *Divided Dish with center handle, 15"l; double figural portraits of Women Holding Roses; turquoise background; gold stencilled designs; ES Mark 13.*

Plate 620. Plate, 9½"d; figural scenic decor of "Portia and Shylock" (marked on left side); "Walter Paget" signature on right. Scene is from Shakespeare's Merchant of Venice; wide gold tapestry border with turquoise beading and floral reserves; ES Mark 14; rare decoration.

Plate 621. Plate, 9¼"d; Shakespeare figural scene, "Death of King Lear" (marked on left side) with signature of "Walter Paget" on right side; gold tapestry finish; ES Mark 14; rare decoration.

Plate 622. Plate, 9¼"d; a third figural scene in the Shakespeare series, "Falstaff & Mrs. Ford" (marked on left side) with "H.M.P." initials on right side; gold tapestry finish with turquoise beading matching other two plates; ES Mark 14; rare decoration.

220

Plate 623. *Plate; portrait of Marie with cameos of Madame Récamier, Napoleon, and Josephine around outer border; gold stencilled floral chains; ES Mark 14.*

Plate 624. *Divided Dish with center handle, a companion to the piece shown in Plate 623; ES Mark 14.*

Plate 625. *Set of Cups, 3¼"h, and Saucers; Napoleon, and Josephine portraits; turquoise finish; floral reserves; gold stencilled floral chains; ES Mark 11.*

Plate 626. *Plate, 7¾"d; Gibson girl portrait; gold beaded frame; dark cobalt blue border with gold stencilled floral designs; ES Mark 14.*

Plate 627. *Tray with pierced handles, 11½"l; figural decor of two women and a man holding flowers and a hat; wine finish; ES Mark 14.*

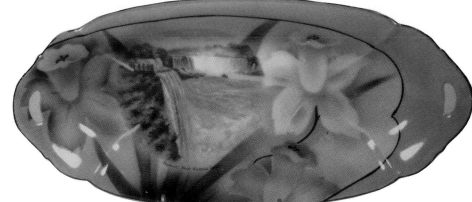

Plate 628. *Celery Dish, 12"l; Souvenir china illustrating Niagara Falls; ES Mark 14.*

Plate 630. *One handled Bowl, 7¼"l x 5⅝"w; Hunting scene; spattered orange finish on bottom of bowl and at top of trees; ES Mark 15.*

Plate 629. *Bowl, 8"l; Coach scene with horse drawn coach, driver, and riders; ES Mark 14.*

Plate 631. Compote, 4¼"h x 8"d; figural lion heads and paws form legs of compote; Dresden Flowers decorate center; small rose buds scattered around inner border with an oval floral reserve on black background; gold trim; ES Mark 12; rare object.

Plate 632. Another view of Compote in Plate 631.

Plate 633. Plate; brilliantly colored Rooster and Chickens decorate center; green grass; enameled gold oak leaves and acorns; green outer border; iridescent finish; ES Mark 14 in blue.

Plate 634. Bowl, 3"h x 9"w, leaf shaped mold around border; large pink lilies on inner border; tinted green outer border; ES Mark 14.

Plate 635. *Plate, 10"d, 8 sided; pink roses; wine outer border; gold stencilled designs; ES Mark 14.*

Plate 636. *Bowl, 11¼"d, scalloped and beaded mold, pierced handles; multicolored pansies with enameled centers; gold stencilled designs; pearl luster outer border; ES Mark 10 (without numbers).*

Plate 637. *Bowl, 11"d; scalloped border with undecorated jewels in shields between scallops extending toward center of bowl; red and white roses; iridescent blue and brown finish on border; ES Mark 14.*

Plate 639. *Plate, 6"d; pink and orange tulips; ES Mark 15.*

Plate 638. *Celery Dish, 12"l; clusters of small white lilies; ES Mark 14.*

Plate 640. *Plate, 8½"d; pink and white wild roses; blue tinted finish; ES Mark 14.*

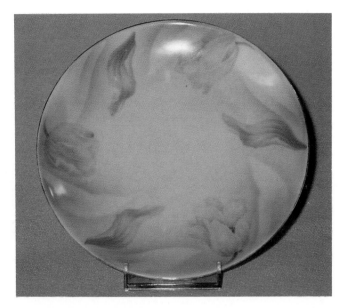

Plate 641. *Bowl, 5¾"d; pink and white tulips with large green leaves around outer border; ES Mark 15.*

Plate 643. *Plate, 5¾"d; white tulips in a stylized design; ES Mark 15.*

Plate 642. *Plate, 7½"d; scenic decor of bird, lake, and trees; ES Mark 15.*

Plate 644. *Tray, 8¼" x 11¼"; large yellow roses with enameled work around outer border; black lines around outer border and forming a rectangle design in center of tray; ES Mark 15.*

225

Plate 646. *Salt and Pepper Shakers; pink flowers; ES Mark 14.*

Plate 645. *Covered Sugar Bowl, 3"h, and Creamer, 2¾"h; large pink roses; ES Mark 14.*

Plate 647. *Cup, 2"h, and Saucer; pink and white wild roses; ES Mark 14.*

Plate 648. *Covered Sugar Bowl, 5"h, and Creamer, 3¾"h; orchids on white to beige background; ES Mark 14.*

Plate 649. Covered Sugar Bowl, Creamer, Salt and Pepper Shakers, Toothpick Holder, Vase with Frog. These pieces are decorated with the same background coloring. The Flower Holder with Frog and the Creamer have a Masted Ship scene with a Lighthouse in background; the other pieces, except for one Shaker, have a Windmill and Village scene; one Shaker has a different Village scene; ES Mark 14.

Plate 650. Chocolate Pot, 8¾"h, pedestal base; large red roses in reserve on front; green finish with gold stencilled designs; ES Mark 14.

Plate 651. Chocolate Set: Pot, 9"h; Cups, 3"h, and Saucers; large yellow roses on tinted lavender to white background; gold stencilled designs; ES Mark 14.

Plate 652. *Ink Well, 3⅞"h; mythological scene with large roses forming border around middle; ES Mark 12.*

Plate 653. *Pin Box, 2⅝"d; basket of pink roses; gold trim; ES Mark 12.*

Plate 654. *Covered Box; 2½"h x 5¼"d; pink rose with smaller flowers; ES Mark 12.*

Plate 655. *Covered Box, 3"h x 5¼"d; mythological figural scene decorates lid; pink roses and gold stencilled designs around borders; ES Mark 12.*

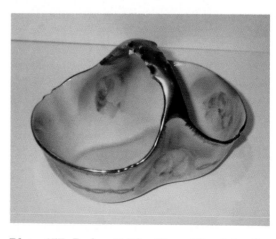

Plate 656. *Covered Box, 2½"h x 4½"w; mythological figural scene of two women and a cherub; ornate gold stencilled work around inner border of lid; small floral pattern around outer border; ES Mark 12.*

Plate 657. *Basket, 6½"l x 4"w x 4"h; pink tulips; gold trim around border; handle painted gold; ES Mark 14.*

228

Plate 658. *Vase, 11"h; Lady With Doves figural decor; gold beaded frame; ES Mark 14.*

Plate 660. *Vase, 8"h; figural portrait of woman with pink roses in her hair; iridescent Tiffany finish around portrait and on neck of vase; turquoise beaded work on gold background decorates body; ES Mark 14.*

Plate 659. *Vase, 9½"h; figural portrait of Woman Holding One Rose; tinted rose finish shading to wine at base; ES Mark 13.*

Plate 661. *Vase, 8"h; portrait of Woman Holding Flowers; wine finish overlaid with gold stencilled designs; pearl luster finish on top border and foot of base; gold handles; ES Mark 14.*

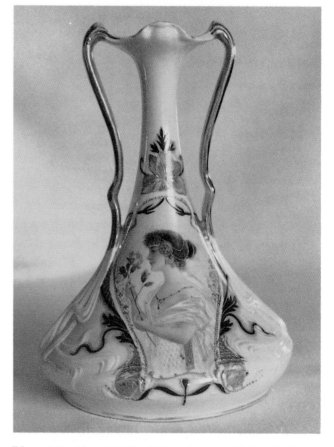

Plate 662. *Vase 11¾"h, 8"d at base, molded swirl designs on body; Woman Holding One Rose figural portrait; gold embellishments; ES Mark 14.*

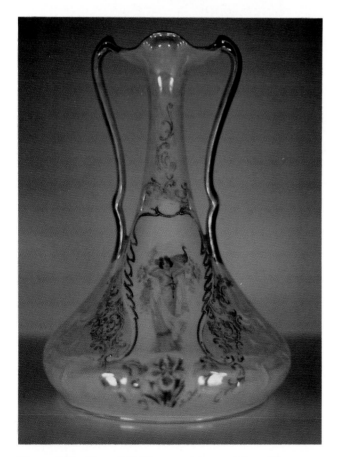

Plate 663. *Vase, 11¾"h, matching mold in Plate 662; Lady With Peacock, gold stencilled and beaded designs; pearl luster finish; gold handles; ES Mark 13.*

Plate 664. Pair of Lamps made from Ewers, 22"h; portrait of woman with red flowers in hair on left, and portrait of woman with pink roses in hair on right; wine finish with gold framing and stencilled designs; light green pearl luster band at base of neck and on interior; ES Mark 12.

Plate 665. Lamp made from vase; portrait of woman holding hand over eyes; gold stencilled designs on cream body; ES mark not visible because of lamp base.

Plate 666. Ewer, 17"h; mythological scenes on front and back, two views of women with cherub; turquoise finish on neck and base; gold stencilled floral designs; gold handles; ES Mark 14.

Plate 667. Reverse of Ewer in Plate 666.

Beehive Marks

A Beehive distinguished by a "dot" is attributed to the E.S. factory. This particular Beehive is found as part of one Prov Sxe mark (see Prov Sxe Mark 6). The ES Beehive mark was printed in green or blue. The decoration on pieces with this mark consists chiefly of allegorical, mythical, or pastoral scenes. The borders are decorated in rich wine reds, cobalt blues, or deep greens. Shapes are simple, along classical lines. The Beehive mark evidently was not meant actually to imitate the mark used by the Royal Porcelain Factory in Vienna. The "dot" would not have been added to the mark if that had been the intention. The mark seems to reflect a style of decoration which was similar to that used by the Royal company.

There has not been any specific time period listed by references for this Beehive mark. It probably overlapped the Prov Sxe marks because it does comprise part of one version of those marks. The O.S. factory also used similar shapes and decorations as those found with this Beehive mark. That factory was not established until 1892, and thus a logical time period for the ES Beehive mark seems to be during the early 1900s to the 1920s. (The O.S. Factory used a different Beehive mark; see section on O.S. Marks.) A few pieces with the ES Beehive mark are decorated with floral designs similar to those found on R.S. Germany and R.S. Tillowitz marked china. All of the examples shown here were found by Mr. Capers in Germany. Evidently few, if any, ES Beehive marked pieces were exported to this country.

ES Mark 18, Beehive in green or blue.

ES Mark 19, Beehive in green or blue with inventory numbers.

Plate 678. *Cup and Saucer; mythological scene of three women and a cherub on interior of cup; floral reserves on saucer; yellow-gold inner border with elaborate gold stencilled work; ES Mark 18 in green.*

Plate 679. Pair of Cups and Saucers decorated with mythological scenes; wine and green finishes on borders; ES Mark 18 in green.

Plate 680. Cup and Saucer decorated like set in Plate 678 except inner border is bright blue; ES Mark 18 in green.

Plate 681. Cup and Saucer decorated with a different mythological scene on cup's interior; green finish on inner border; ES Mark 18 in green.

235

Plate 682. Cups and Saucers (3 sets); floral reserves around interior of cup and saucer; wine finish; gold stencilled designs; ES Mark 18 in green.

Plate 683. Cups and Saucers (3 sets); bright multicolored flowers; gold stencilled border designs; ES Mark 18 in green.

Plate 684. Vase, 5¾"h x 3"w; mythological scene of chariot, women, and cherubs; detailed gold stencilled designs; border of pink roses around top of vase; ES Mark 18 in green.

Plate 685. Vase, 8⅞"h; two women with a cherub figural decor; floral and gold stencilled border designs; red frame and bands accent vase; gold handles; ES Mark 19.

Plate 686. Vase, 6½"h, 3 legs on applied base; seated women with cherub figural decor; cobalt blue finish; gold beaded frame; pink roses form border around top; ES Mark 18 in blue.

236

Plate 687. Tray, 15⅝"l x 6"w; mythological scene of white horses, angel, and men; wine colored inner border with floral reserves; gold stencilled designs over surface; ES Mark 18.

Plate 688. Tray, 19"l x 6⅝"w; two seated women with cherub; green outer border separated by wine panels with rose and gold wreath floral designs; ES Mark 18 in green.

Plate 689. Vase, 12¼"h; figural scenes based on Angelica Kaufmann's work decorate front and back; wine finish at top and base with green bands; surface covered with gold stencilled designs; "A. Kaufmann" printed on front indicating origin of original painting on which transfer was based; ES Mark 18 in blue.

Plate 690. Reverse of Vase in Plate 689.

237

Plate 691. Divided Dish with handle and three sections, 7¾" x 7¾"; mixed fruit decor; ES Mark 18 in green.

Plate 692. Double Candle Holders, 6¾"h x 4⅝"w; multicolored flowers scattered across surface; gold trim; ES Mark 18 in green.

Plate 693. Vase, 8"h; a large pink and a large white flower; gold stippled background; green and blue floral border at top and base; ES Mark 18 in green.

Plate 694. Vase, 8"h; large white lilies with light pink tint; ES Mark 18 in green.

Other E.S. Marks

While the Royal Saxe and Prov Sxe marks are the ones most frequently found for the E.S. production on the American market, a few other marks also were used. Most of the examples are simply shaped. The decoration is floral, along R.S. Germany lines. The time period for these several marks would be during the 1920s to early 1930s. In this section, the particular mark is shown first, followed by examples with the mark. One mark, an ES monogram mark (see ES Mark 25) does not have an example. The mark was shown by Hartwich (1984) as one of the marks used by the E.S. factory.

ES Mark 20, "Erdmann Schlegelmilch, Thuringia, Hand-painted" in script form.

Plate 695. One Handled Dish or Nappy, 6"d; Dogwood blossoms; gold stencilled pattern around border; ES Mark 20.

Plate 696. Cup, 2"h, and Saucer; Dogwood pattern as shown in Plate 695; ES Mark 20.

Plate 697. Covered Sugar Bowl, 2¾"h, and Creamer, 2¾"h; large white and pink flowers with enameled centers; gold stippled work; ES Mark 20.

ES Mark 21, "E. Schlegelmilch, Germany, Handpainted" in script form.

Plate 698. Chop Plate, 11¾"d; orange poppies in a stylized design; ES Mark 20.

Plate 699. Plate, 6"d; stylized peach and white flowers; ES Mark 21.

Plate 700. Bowl, 9"d; pink and white tulips; ES Mark 21.

ES Mark 22, "Prussian China" printed over banner with "Suhl" and "Germany" below banner.

Plate 701. *Mayonnaise Dish, 5"d, and Ladle; floral border; ES Mark 22.*

Plate 702. *Plate, 8½"d; pink, orange, and white tulips; ES Mark 22.*

Plate 703. *Dresser Set: Tray, 11"l; Hair Receiver, 3½"h x 4"d; Covered Powder Jar, 3½"h x 4"d, footed; pink tulips with enameled work; ES Mark 22.*

ES Mark 23, Crown over ellipse mark with "Schlegelmilch, 1861, Suhl" printed inside ellipse; "Hand-painted" in script below mark.

Plate 704. Compote, 4⅛"h x 10"w; figural decor of couple in garden, colonial dress; dark blue cobalt finish around portrait; gold beaded frame with gold stencilled designs; ES Mark 23.

ES Mark 24, ES initials in monogram form.

ES Mark 25, ES initials divided by a curved line.

Plate 705. Small Decorative Plate, 3"d, pierced work around border; two seated women with cherub figural decor; gold finish; ES Mark 24.

Plate 706. Plate matching one in Photograph 705 with another view of the figures.

242

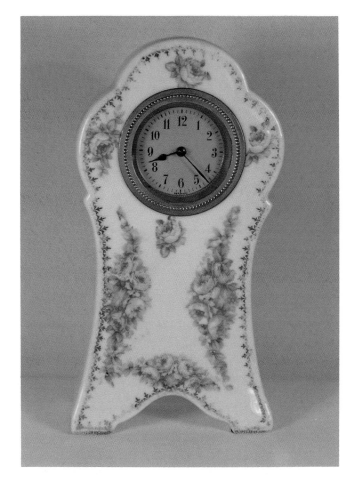

Plate **707.** *Clock, 8"h; pink rose garlands decorate front with a wreath of pink roses on back (not shown); ES Mark 24.*

Plate **708.** *Plate, 10½"d; clusters of lilac colored flowers with center design outlined in green with floral garlands on three sides; ES Mark 24.*

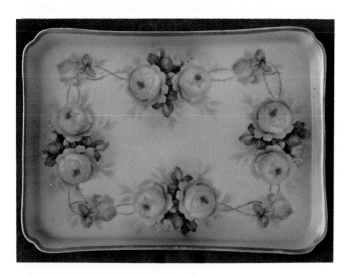

Plate **709.** *Dresser Tray; large white roses with yellow-orange centers; ES Mark 24.*

Plate **710.** *Chocolate Set: Pot, 10"h; Cups, 3"h, and Saucers; large pink roses with lily of the valley; high glossy finish; beaded floral finial; gold trim; ES Mark 24.*

243

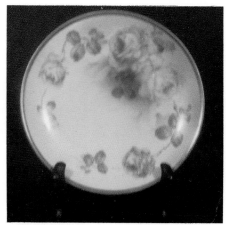

ES Mark 26, Bird in shield with Crown above and "Prussia" below, in green.

Plate 711. Plate, 6"d; pink and white roses; gold trim; ES Mark 26.

Plate 712. Potpourri Jar, 5"h, footed; handpainted violets (not factory decoration); ES Mark 26.

Plate 713. Syrup Pitcher, 4"h; pink and white roses; ES Mark 26.

Plate 714. Covered Sugar Bowl, 5"h and Creamer, 3¾"h; white roses with a peach tint and enameled work; gold trim; ES Mark 26.

Plate 716. Vase, 6¾"h; figural courting scene; wine and green borders around center decor; gold stencilled designs; multicolored flowers decorate top and base; ES Mark 26.

Plate 715. Hair Receiver, pink roses; ES Mark 26.

Ambiguous Marks, Molds, and Decorations

To conclude this part on the Erdmann Schlegelmilch Factory, a few marks, molds, and decoration transfers are shown which seem to be related to that factory, although these pieces do not have a documented ES mark. Like the section on Ambiguous Marks which followed R.S. Schlegelmilch Marks and Photographs, this section has been included as a study segment. By showing such examples, perhaps more information will surface to explain the reason for the similarities between these examples and E.S. china.

The first mark is a monogram which at first glance seems to contain the letter "R." The mark, however, is really impossible to decipher clearly. Two examples were found with the mark. One is a vase made in a definite ES shape. It is also decorated with an ES transfer, "Lady with Peacock." Another vase with the mark has a simple ovoid shape. It is decorated with a portrait of the "Woman with Holly Wreath," also a transfer found on ES marked china.

The second ambiguous mark is an embossed Star. It is like Star Mark 2 shown earlier. The mold of the base is the same ES mold discussed above with ambiguous Mark 1. Windmill decorations are found on ES marked china, but this transfer is not identical to any of those (see Plate 501 in G1, Plates 494 and 496 in G2, and Plate 649 in this section for ES windmill designs).

Mark 3 contains the initials "E.Z." with "Clarmont, Germany." Two ES molds are shown with this mark. One decoration transfer is identified with ES marks (Lady with Swallows), see Plate 720a. The portrait on the vase in Plate 720, however, is the same as one shown in Plate 225 of the *Third Series*. That piece has an RSP mark.

The last ambiguous mark is composed of wings inside a circle combined with the works "Clarus Ware." The mold is unlike any ES mold. The decoration is the familiar "Lady with Peacock," a popular ES transfer decoration.

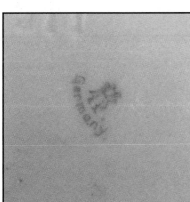

Ambiguous Monogram Mark with "Germany" in green.

Plate 717. Vase, 9"h, ES Germany Mold (see Plate 685); Lady with Peacock figural decor (ES transfer); Ambiguous Monogram Mark.

Plate 718. Vase, 4¾"h, salesman's sample; Woman with Holly Wreath in Hair (ES transfer); Ambiguous Monogram Mark.

Embossed 8 point Star Mark, similar to Star Mark 2 (see earlier section on Ambiguous Marks following Reinhold Schlegelmilch Marks and Photographs).

Plate 719. *Vase, 6⅛"h, ES Germany Mold (see Plate 685); Windmill scenic decor; Embossed 8 point Star Mark.*

EZ Clarmont Germany Mark.

Plate 720. *Vase, 8½"h, ES Germany Mold (see Plate 480 in the Second Series); portrait of woman with pink flowers in her hair (see Plate 225 in Third Series); wine finish with gold designs framing portrait; pearl green luster finish at top of neck; gold handles; EZ Clarmont Mark.*

Plate 720a. *Three Vases: Pair, 10¼"h, ES Mold; portrait reserves of Women Holding Flowers; green pearl luster finish; gold trim. Center: three handled Vase, 12"h; Lady with Swallows; green pearl luster finish; gold trim; EZ Clarmont Mark on each vase.*

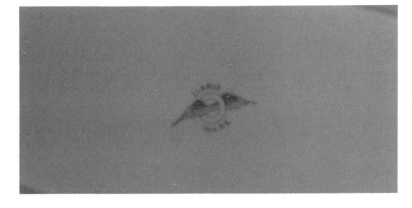

Clarus Ware Mark.

Plate 721. Celery Dish, deeply scalloped mold with large floral designs; Lady with Peacock decor (ES transfer); pearl luster finish; heavy gold work on border; Clarus Ware Mark.

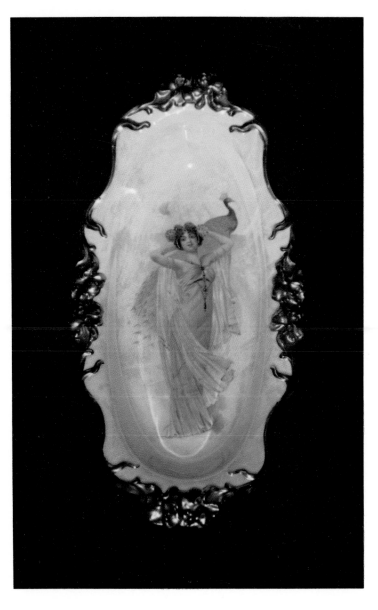

Oscar Schlegelmilch Marks and Photographs

Comparison of Dating Information for OS Marks		
Mark	*Röntgen (1980)*	*Zühlsdorff (1988)*
Beehive	after 1892	1891 – 1930
OS Monogram	1896 –	1896 – 1928
OS St. Kilian/Germany	1904	1900
Crown, alone	after 1930	1900 – 1930
Crown with L	1900 – 1957	after 1900
Crown over L	1950 – 1972	1930 –

Below is my suggested chronology and time periods for the OS Marks.

Chronology for OS Marks	
Beehive	after 1892 to 1920s (overlapping with other OS marks)
OS Monogram	by 1910 (shown in Ceramic Address Book for that year)
OS St. Kilian/Germany	early 1900s to 1930s
Crown alone	time unclear, but it could precede the Crown with L mark
Crown with L	circa 1920s to 1930s
Crown over L	circa 1950s to early 1970s

Examples of Oscar Schlegelmilch's marks and china were not included in my first edition, but a few marks and photographs of china were presented in my *Second Series*. The OS marks do not easily fit into specific years. Danckert does not show any dates for the OS marks. The dates listed by Röntgen and Zühlsdorff differ widely for some of the OS marks. Above is a chart showing those differences.

The Beehive mark would not have been as early as 1891, as shown by Zühlsdorff. The company was not founded until 1892. The OS St. Kilian/Germany marks are given a similar beginning time, the early 1900s, by both references. The OS monogram mark is shown by both to have been used from 1896. That particular mark has not been available on a piece to be photographed. The Crown with L mark is noted as being after 1900 by both sources, and Röntgen shows 1957 as the last year of its use. The Crown mark alone is listed as in use after 1930 by Röntgen, but Zühlsdorff shows the mark's use between 1900 and 1930. A similar time discrepancy between the two sources is for the Crown over L mark. Röntgen shows the mark used between 1950 and 1972, while Zühlsdorff lists the mark as beginning in 1930.

Mark 1, the OS monogram mark, is listed by Röntgen (1980: 308) to have been used from 1896. No examples with that mark were available for this edition. Mark 4, the St. Kilian Mark, was in use from 1904. It is possible that the Beehive mark was instituted sometime between 1892 and 1904 (see OS Mark 2). In fact, it is possible that the Beehive mark was one of the first marks implemented by the O.S. Factory. Since the Erdmann Schlegelmilch factory used a Beehive mark, and Oscar had been associated with that factory prior to establishing the Langeweisen pottery, such a mark would have been only natural. There is a strong resemblance between the OS and ES Beehives. The OS Beehive is found in black as well as green. It is a little more ambiguous, however, because it does not have as distinguishing a characteristic as the "dot" in the ES Beehive mark. The lines in the OS mark are shown by some references to be a bit crooked or "wavy," but the marks shown here have straight lines. (See OS Marks 2 and 3.)

Mark 3 appears to be a transition mark with both the Beehive and St. Kilian marks. The Coburg Ceramic Directory for 1910 indicates that Mark 3 (OS monogram) and Mark 4 (St. Kilian) were in use at that time. The Beehive mark is not shown for the factory, thus the Beehive mark could date between 1892 and 1910.

Mark 5 is a variation of Mark 4, and is apparently a later mark. It includes the words "Porzellan Fabrik Langeweisen." Mark 6 could be the first "Crown" type mark for the factory. It might have been used after Mark 5 because the wording is similar.

The time periods for the gold Crown marks 7 through 10 are not clear. I suggest that they are after Mark 6. The shapes of the crowns vary. It is conceivable that the single Crown marks were used before the Crown with "L" marks.

Mark 11 is obviously a more modern mark than the others. The late 1950s to early 1970s, as listed by Röntgen (1980: 158), seems logical. Mark 12 is a porcelain advertising sign for the factory.

The decoration on O.S. china is very similar to the E.S. portrait and figural themes. The latter is predominantly mythical or allegorical. The molds are classical in shape and do not reflect the Art Nouveau styles used by the E.S. factory, however. Some of the floral transfers are more kin to decoration found on china which has other German or Bavarian marks.

A few unmarked items are included at the end of this section. The molds and decorations seem to fit the OS image rather than any other type of Schlegelmilch china.

OS Mark 1, initials in monogram form.

OS Mark 2, Beehive in black or green.

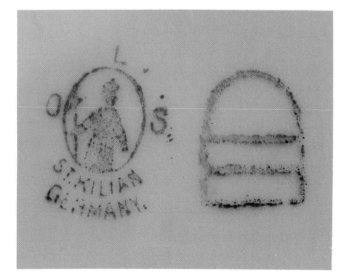

OS Mark 3, St. Kilian, Germany with Beehive, in green.

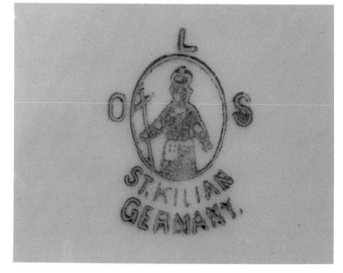

OS Mark 4, St. Kilian Germany in green.

OS Mark 5, St. Kilian in a circle with "Porzellan Fabrik Langewiesen," and "Germany" printed below circle.

OS Mark 6, Crown in circle with "Porzellan Fabrik Langewiesen," in red.

OS Mark 7, Crown with "L" in gold.

OS Mark 8, same as mark 7 with "Handgemalt" (Handpainted) in gold.

OS Mark 9, Crown in gold (variation in shape from crown in Marks 6, 7, 10, and 11).

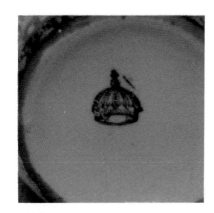

OS Mark 10, Crown in gold (variation in shape from crown in Marks 6 through 9, and 11).

OS Mark 11, Crown and "L" with "Oscar Schlegelmilch" in blue.

OS Mark 12, porcelain advertising sign for the OS factory.

Plate 722. Pair of Vases, 9¾"h; "The Cage" figural decor (based on a painting by Boucher); wine and green highlights with gold accents; OS Mark 2 in black.

Plate 723. Cup and Saucer Sets; Napoleon portrait decorates interior of cups; wine and green accents with gold stencilled designs; OS Mark 2 in black.

Plate 724. Cake Plate, 11"d; mythological figural decor of dancing women, a man, and cherubs; wine and green borders with gold stencilled floral designs on reserves around outer border; OS Mark 3.

Plate 725. Chocolate Set: Pot, 10½"h; Cups and Saucers; mythical figural scenes decorate center medallions; gold beaded framework; wine finish overlaid with gold stencilled designs; heavy gold trim; OS Mark 3.

Plate 726. *Plate, 10"d; Water Nymph figural decor; green panels around inner border separated by wine diamond shapes; gold stencilled designs; OS Mark 3.*

Plate 727. *Cake Plate, 10¼"d; Lady With Dog figural decor; green finish around inner and outer borders; intricate gold stencilled designs; heavy gold trim; "Gainsborough" printed in lower right corner, indicating original artist's work on which transfer was based; OS Mark 4.*

Plate 728. *Plate, 11½"d; Monk Eating Dinner figural scene; dark green border with gold stencilled designs; OS Mark 4.*

Plate 729. *Plate, 8¼"d; portrait of an Oriental Woman with Fan; dark green border with gold accents; beaded work around portrait; OS Mark 4.*

Plate 730. *Plate, 10"d; mythical scene of girl with scarf and cherub; dark blue-green border; OS Mark 4.*

Plate 731. *Vase, 7"h x 7"w at base; Queen Louise portrait; wine iridescent accents; gold beaded work around portrait; leaf design finished in gold; OS Mark 4.*

Plate 732. *Covered Jar, 2½"h x 2½"d; Dresden Flowers floral design; OS Mark 4.*

Plate 733. *Cake Plate, 10"d; large dark pink roses; gold stencilled designs decorate heavily scalloped outer borders; OS Mark 4.*

Plate 734. *Wall Plaque, 8½"d; pink roses; iridescent finish at top of plaque; gold trim; OS Mark 4.*

Plate 735. Wall Plaque, 11"d; sledding scene decorates center with other outdoor scenes illustrated around inner border: (clockwise) skiing, ice skating, mountain climbing, and tennis; gold trim; OS Mark 5, rare mark, rare decoration.

Plate 738. Covered Box, 1¾"h x 3¾"d, six sided; red and gold designs with red borders; OS Mark 6.

Plate 736. Vase, 8"h; Windmill scenic decor on front with a large multi-storied building on reverse side; iridescent gold finish; OS Mark 4.

Plate 737. Reverse of Vase in Plate 736.

Plate 739. Vase, 7¾"h; small flowers scattered over body; gold trim; OS Mark 7.

Plate 740. *Vase, 6¼"h; multicolored flowers decorate body with a similar floral pattern around top border; gold trim; OS Mark 7.*

Plate 741. *Tea Set with portrait decor: Tray, 15" x 11", King Louis XIV (based on work by Gueslin); Covered Sugar Bowl, 5¼"h with same decor as Tray; Teapot, 6¾"h, King Louis XIV (from work by Joseph Biza); Creamer, 5¼"h, Duchess de Montespair (from work by Rizand); Cup, 3¾"h, Marie Antoinette (from work by Madame LeBrun); Cup, 3¾"h, Madame DuBarry (from work by Higrand). The names of the subjects as well as the artist of the original paintings are printed below the portraits. German Eagles form all finials and handles and spout of Teapot; OS Mark 7 (with the Crown over the "L") in gold on Teapot and Creamer; in reddish-brown on Tray, Sugar Bowl, and one Cup; in red-orange on one Cup; rare set.*

Plate 742. *Cup, 1¾"h, and Saucer; classical figural scene; cobalt blue borders; gold stencilled designs; OS Mark 7.*

Plate 743. *Cup and Saucer decorated with figural classical scene; OS Mark 7.*

Plate 744. *Set of Butter Pats, 3⅛"d; red-orange abstract floral design; gold trim; OS Mark 7.*

Plate 745. *Cup and Saucer; classical figural scene; wine borders; gold stencilled patterns on inner borders; OS Mark 9.*

Plate 746. *Vase, 6"h; recessed panels around base; turquoise and gold decor on white body; OS Mark 8.*

Plate 747. *Pair of Vases, 4½"h, salesman's samples; mythical figural scenes; wine finish on frames around portraits with beaded work and gold stencilled designs; OS Mark 10.*

Plate 748. *Clock, 5¾"h x 3¾"w; figural pastoral cameo on frame with small multicolored flowers on body; gold trim; OS Mark 10.*

Plate 749. *Vase, 3⅛"h, salesman's sample; American Ringneck Pheasant decor (rare decoration); OS Mark 10.*

Plate 750. Cup and Saucer Sets; multicolored floral pattern in center of each cup and on reserve on border; wine and blue finishes; OS Mark 11.

Plate 751. Cup and Saucer; figural decor on interior of cup of couple in eighteenth century dress dancing; wine finish; OS Mark 11 with "Import" printed in gold.

Plate 752. Covered Sugar Bowl, 3¼"h, and Creamer, 3¼"h; classical figural scenes; wide blue bands; gold stencilled designs; OS Mark 11 with "Import" in gold.

Plate 753. Set of Cups and Saucers with multicolored floral pattern around borders; gold stencilled designs; OS Mark 11.

Plate 754. Teapot, 3"h x 5"w; small flowers scattered over body; OS Mark 11 with "Import" in gold.

Plate 756. Pair of Bud Vases, 1"h x 1"w x 2¾"l; small flowers; gold trim; OS Mark 7 (with the Crown over the "L") on one and OS Mark 11 on the other.

Plate 755. Bowl, 11½"d; lavender flowers outlined in gold around inner border on turquoise background; OS Mark 11 with "Handgemalt" (Handpainted).

Plate 757. Console Set: Pair of Candle Holders, 3"h; Vase, 2¼"h x 2½"d; molded body designs highlighted in gold; OS Mark 11.

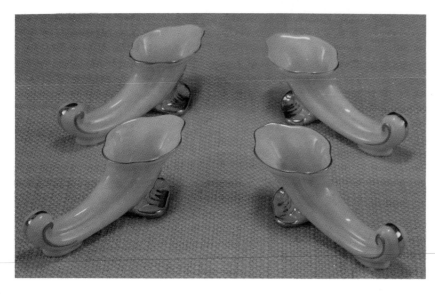

Plate 758. Set of Bud Vases, 3½"l x 1½"w x 1⅜"h; gold trim on white body; OS Mark 11.

Plate 759. Demi-tasse Set: Pot, Covered Sugar Bowl, Creamer, and Cups and Saucers; gold band decor with gold stencilled pattern; OS Mark 11.

Plate 760. Child's Toy Tea Set: Pot, 5¾"h; Covered Sugar Bowl, 3½"h; Creamer, 3⅜"h; small flowers scattered over body; pearl luster finish; OS Mark 11.

Plate 761. Wall Plate, 11½"d, pierced for hanging; mythological scene of women, cherub, and beast; OS Mark 4.

Plate 762. Platter, 11⅞"d; mythological scene, "Venus with Neptune"; beaded and enameled gold work around star shaped frame outlining center scene; unmarked (OS transfer).

Plate 763. Tea Set: Teapot, 6½"h; Covered Sugar Bowl, 3½"h; Creamer, 3"h; Cups and Saucers; figural portraits of women and cherubs with a nautical theme; wine finish overlaid with gold stencilled designs; unmarked.

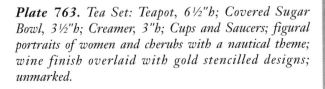

Carl Schlegelmilch Marks and Photographs

The history of the Carl Schlegelmilch factory was presented in the *Third Series*. German references on marks do not show any marks for the company which reflect the initials "C." and "S." Most marks such references show are those used by the successors to the C.S. factory, such as Matthes and Ebel.

Only one mark, with the initials "C." and "S." has been found on examples in the United States. That mark is a clover leaf with the initials "C." and "S." over "Prussia." This particular mark has been erroneously attributed to the O.S. factory by the Germany references. I discussed this error on page 15 in the *Third Series*.

I would suggest that the C.S. Mark was used between 1882 and 1912. That time includes the years when Carl Schlegelmilch was the only owner of the factory. Several relatives of Carl were associated with the factory after 1912 until 1919, when the factory closed. Robert Matthes took over the factory in that year. (A few examples with marks are shown in an Appendix for the Matthes and Ebel factory, successor to Matthes and Co., see page 272.)

The C.S. Mark is found in green or blue. Examples with this mark are seldom found on the American market. The style and decoration of the china are very similar to R.S. Germany and R.S. Tillowitz marked china.

CS Mark 1, clover leaf and initials with "Prussia" in green.

CS Mark 2, the same as Mark 1 with "Hand-Painted," in blue or green.

Plate 764. *Covered Sugar Bowl, 4"h; Creamer, 3"h; hand-painted yellow roses, artist signed "Edith Belleforsy" (non-factory decoration); CS Mark 1.*

Plate 765. *Plate, 7¾"d; large white poppies with enameled work; gold beaded outer rim; gold stencilled designs on inner and outer borders; CS Mark 2 in green.*

Plate 766. Hair Receiver, 2½"h x 4"d; dogwood blossoms with holly and red berries; CS Mark 1.

Plate 767. Plate, 9"d; pink roses in a stylized design; gold trim; CS Mark 2 in blue.

Plate 768. Cake Plate, 11"d; small pink roses with gold stencilled garlands in center and around border; CS Mark 1.

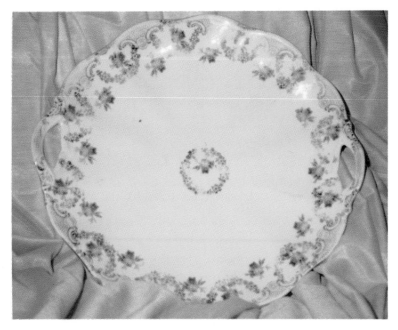

Bibliography

Adressbuch der Keram-Industrie. Coburg: Müller & Schmidt, 1893, 1910, 1913, 1930, 1932, 1934, 1937, 1941, 1949.

Ananoff, Alexandre, *L'oeuvre Dessiné* de Francois Boucher. Paris: F. De Nobele, Librarie, 1966.

Barber, Edwin Atlee, *The Ceramic Collectors' Glossary.* New York: Da Capo Press, 1967.

Barlock, George E. and Eileen. *The Treasures of R.S. Prussia,* 1976.

Bartran, Margaret. *A Guide to Color Reproductions.* Second Edition. Metuchen, NJ: The Scarecrow Press, Inc., 1971.

Bearne, Mrs. *A Court Painter and His Circle, Francois Boucher.* London: Adelphi Terrace, 1913.

Benson, E.F. *The White Eagle of Poland.* New York: George H. Doran Company, n.d.

Boger, Louise Ade. *The Dictionary of World Pottery and Porcelain.* New York: Charles Scribner's Sons, 1971.

Buell, Raymond Leslie. *Poland: Key to Europe.* London: Jonathan Cape, 1939.

Calvert, Albert F. (ed.). *Murillo: The Spanish Series.* London: John Lane, The Bodley Head Gallery, MCMVII.

Capers, R.H. Discussions with Gerhard Soppa, November 26 and 27, 1991.

_____. "R.S. Made in (German) Poland" Mark, *R.S. Prussia* (Number 16, February, 1992): 8-10.

Castries, Duc de. *Madame Récamier.* Hachette, 1971.

Catalogue of Reproductions of Paintings Prior to 1860. Paris: UNESCO, 1972.

Chaffers, William. *Handbook of Marks and Monograms on Pottery and Porcelain.* Revised edition. London: William Reeves, 1968.

_____. *Marks & Monograms on Pottery and Porcelain.* Vol. 1, 15th Revised edition. London: William Reeves, 1965.

Chrościcki, Leon. *Porcelana — Znaki Wytworni Europejskich.* Warszawa: Wybawnictwo Artystyczno-Graficzne, 1974.

Cox, W.E. *The Book of Pottery and Porcelain.* Vol. 1. New York: L. Lee Shepard Co., Inc., 1944.

Cushion, J.P. *Pocket Book of German Ceramic Marks and Those of Other Central European Countries.* London: Faber and Faber, 1961.

Cushion, J.P. (in collaboration with W.B. Honey). *Handbook of Pottery and Porcelain Marks.* London: Faber & Faber, 1956.

Danckert, Ludwig. *Handbuch des Europäischen Porzellans.* Munich: Prestel Verlag, 1954, 1967, 1978, 1984, 1992.

Day, William E. *Blue Book of Art Values.* Third Edition. Paducah, KY: Collector Books, 1979.

Dyboski, Roman. *Outlines of Polish History.* London: George Allen & Unwin, Ltd. Revised edition, 1931.

Encyclopedia Britannica. Vol. 18. Chicago: William Benton, 1970.

Fayard, Artheme (ed.). *Souvenirs De Mme. Louise Elisabeth Vigee-LeBrun.* Paris: F. Funch-Bretana.

Gaston, Mary Frank. *The Collector's Encyclopedia of Limoges Porcelain.* Paducah, KY: Collector Books, 1980.

_____. *The Collector's Encyclopedia of R.S. Prussia.* Paducah, KY: Collector Books, 1982.

_____. "Rare R.S. (Schlegelmilch) Marks." *Schroeder's Insider,* December, 1983.

_____. "More Schlegelmilch Marks!" *Schroeder's Insider,* October, 1984.

_____. *The Collector's Encyclopedia of R.S. Prussia,* Second Series. Paducah, KY: Collector Books, 1986.

_____. "Schlegelmilch China: Ambiguous, Scarce, and New Marks." Presentation at the annual meeting of the International Association of R.S. Prussia Collectors, Inc., August, 1991.

Graul, Richard and Albrecht Kurzwelly. *Alt Thüringer Porzellan,* 1909.

Haggar, Reginald G. *The Concise Encyclopedia of Continental Pottery and Porcelain.* New York: Hawthorne Books, Inc., 1960.

Hall, James. *Dictionary of Subjects and Symbols in Art.* Revised edition. New York: Harper & Row, 1979.

Hammond, Dorothy. *Confusing Collectibles.* Des Moines, Iowa: Wallace Homestead, 1969.

Hartwich, Bernd. *The History of the Suhl Porcelain Factories 1861-1937.* Tasked by the Technical School for Museum Caretakers. Leipzig & Weapons Museum, Suhl, Germany, 1984. (Translation by R.H. Capers.)

Hayden, C. Chumley. *Why R.S. Prussia?* Springfield, OR: C. Chumley Hayden, 1970.

Heimatkalender des Kreises Falkenberg (Hometown Almanac for the County of Falkenberg), 1927. (Translation by R. H. Capers.)

Honey, W.B. *German Porcelain.* London: Faber and Faber, MCMXLVII.

Hymanson, Albert M. *A Dictionary of Universal Biography of all Ages and of all People.* Second Edition. New York: E.P. Dutton & Co., Inc. 1951.

"Wilhelm Kahlert." Obituary in *Grottkau-Falkenberger Heimatblatt,* Nr. 24, 1967. (Translation by R.H. Capers.)

Klingenbrunn, Marietta. *Deutsche Porzellanmarken von 1708 bis heute.* Augsburg, Germany: Battenburg Verlag, 1990.

Kovel, Ralph and Terry. *Kovel's New Dictionary of Marks.* New York: Crown Publications, Inc., 1986.

Kraemer, Ekkehard. *Sächsisch-thüringisches Manufakturporzellan,* 1985.

LaRousse Encyclopedia of World Geography. New York: Odyssey Press. Adapted form Geographie Universelle Larousse, Western Publishing Co., 1965.

Lehner, Lois. *Complete Book of American Kitchen and Dinnerware.* Des Moines: Wallace-Homestead, 1980.

_____. *Lehner's Encyclopedia of U.S. Marks on Pottery, Porcelain & Clay.* Paducah, KY: Collector Books, 1988.

Lehr, Margaret Marshall and Margaret Pattie Follet. *A Scrapbook About Old China.* Moorhead, MN: Follett Studios, 1964.

Leistikow-Duchardt, Annelore. *Die Entwicklung eines neuen Stiles im Porzellan.* Heidelberg: Carl Winter Universitatsverlag, 1957.

Lewis, C.T. Courtney. *The Picture Printer of the Nineteenth Century: George Baxter.* London: Sampson Law, Marsten & Co., Ltd. 1911.

Lucas, E.V. *Chardin and Vigee-Lebrun.* London: Methuen & Co., Ltd, .n.d.

McCaslin, Mary. "A Visit to Tillowitz, Poland – A Lot of Surprises." *R.S. Prussia* (Number 18, July 1992): 5-7.

McCaslin, Mary and Robert. "R.S. Prussia Club Restores Schlegelmilch Grave Site." *Antique Week* (July 27, 1992): 12 and 23.

McCaslin, Robert. "Answers From the Past." *R.S. Prussia* (Number 18, July 1992): 8.

Marple, Lee. "Hidden Images." Presentation at the annual meeting of the International Association of R.S. Prussia Collectors, Inc., August, 1991.

Meyers Grosses Konversations-Lexikon. Sixth Edition. Vol 17. Leipzig and Vienna: Biographisches Institut, 1907.

Mountfield, David. *The Antique Collectors' Illustrated Dictionary.* London, Hamlyn, 1974.

Muehsam, Gerd (ed.). *French Painters and Paintings from the Fourteenth Century to Post Impressionism.* New York: Fredrich Ungar Publishing Co., 1970.

Norman, Colleen and Rose Greider. "Identification of Unmarked Pieces." Presentation at the annual meeting of the International Association of R.S. Prussia Collectors, Inc., August, 1991.

Norman, Geraldine. *Nineteenth-Century Painters and Painting: A Dictionary.* Thames and Hudson, 1977.

Pattloch, Franz. "Erinnerung an Tillowitz/Oberschlesien" [Memories of Tillowitz, Upper Silesia]. No date or source for periodical; post World War II refugee publication. (Translated by R. H. Capers.)

Penkala, Maria. *European Porcelain: A Handbook for the Collector.* Second Edition. Rutland, VT: Charles E. Tuttle, 1968.

Poche, Emanuel. *Porcelain Marks of the World.* New York: Arco Publishing Co., Inc., 1974.

Porcelit Tulowicki [Stoneware from Tulowice]. Monograph of the "Tillowice" Porcelit Plant as presented by the Exhibition Office, Opole, June-July 1984. (Translated by Roman Zawada.)

"Porzellan kommt aus OS" [Porcelain Comes out of Upper Silesia]. *Breslauer Neueste Nachrichten* (April 10, 1938). (Translated by R.H. Capers.)

Röntgen, Robert E. *Marks on German, Bohemian and Austrain Porcelain: 1710 to the Present.* Exton, PA: Schiffer Publishing Co., 1981.

Rose, William John. *The Drama of Upper Silesia.* Brattleboro, VT: Stephen Daye Press, 1935.

Schlegelmilch, Clifford J. *Handbook of Erdmann and Reinhold Schlegelmilch, Prussia-Germany and Oscar Schlegelmilch, Germany.* Third Edition, 1973.

Sorenson, Don C. *My Collection R.S. Prussia,* 1979.

Stryienski, Casimir (ed.) *Memoirs of the Countess Potocka.* New York Doubleday & McClure Co., 1901.

Terrell, George W., Jr. *Collecting R.S. Prussia: Identification and Values.* Florence, AL: Books Americana, 1982.

Thalheim, Karl G. and A. Hillen Ziegfeld (eds.). *Der deutsche Osten. Seine Geschichte, sein Wesen und seine Aufgabe.* Berlin: Propylaen, 1936.

The Antique Trader Price Guide to Antiques. Dubuque, IA: Babka Publishing Company, Inc., Summer 1979, Volume X, No.2, Issue No. 32.

The Ceramist. Vol. 3 (Winter Quarter), 1923.

The International Geographic Encyclopedia and Atlas. Boston: Houghton Mifflin Company, 1979.

The World Book Atlas. Field Enterprises Educational Corporation, 1973.

Thorne, J.O. (ed.). *Chambers Biographical Dictionary.* Revised edition. New York: St. Martin's Press, 1969.

Treharne, R.F. and Harold Fullard (eds.). *Muir's Historical Atlas Medieval and Modern.* Tenth Edition. New York: Barnes and Noble, Inc., 1964.

Wandycz, Piotr S. *The Lands of Partitioned Poland, 1795-1918.* Seattle: University of Washington Press, 1923.

Warzecha, Richard. "Ein Besuch in der Tillowitzer Porzellanfabrik" [A Visit to the Tillowitz Porcelain Factory], circa 1953. Publication source unknown. (Translated by R. H. Capers.)

Webster's Biographical Dictionary. Springfield, MA: G. and C. Merriam Company, 1976.

Webster's New Geographical Dictionary. Springfield, MA; G. and C. Merriam Company, 1972.

Weis, Gustav. *Ullstein Porzellanbuch.* Frankfurt, Berlin, Wein: Verlag Ullstein Gimblt, 1975. First Edition, 1964.

Wenke, George. "Tillowitzer Porzellangeschichte." *Unser Oberschlesien* (August 22, 1984). (Translated by R. H. Capers.)

Zühlsdorff, Dieter. *Marken Lexikon – Porzellan und Keramik Report 1885-1935.* Stuttgart: Arnoldsche, 1988.

Appendices
"China Blau" Pattern
Reinhold Schlegelmilch Figurines
Matthes and Ebel Factory
Erdmann Schlegelmilch Family Tree
Death Notices for Julius Schlegelmilch
Erdmann Schlegelmilch Factory Documents

"China Blau" Pattern

Photocopy of a Tea Tile in the "China Blau" pattern. The literal translation of the pattern name is "an Oriental design in blue." This particular item is marked with the initials "RST" arranged vertically within a dotted circle. See R.S. Tillowitz Mark 1 in the section on Reinhold Schlegelmilch Marks and Photographs.

Reinhold Schlegelmilch Figurines

The R.S. Schlegelmilch Factory in Tillowitz manufactured a line of figurines during the 1920s and 1930s. A series of animal figures was based on the designs of Max Rüffler, the son of Gustav Rüffler, the original chief mold maker for the Reinhold Schlegelmilch factory. Wilhelm Kahlert, the son-in-law of Gustav Rüffler, was the chief mold maker at the time the figurines were produced, however. In addition to implementing the animal designs of Max Rüffler, Kahlert is credited with developing another series of figurines based on themes from literature and famous paintings. Such figures are rarely found on the American market. A list of the figures is included here with a few photographs of examples. (Information, List of Figurines, and Pictures of Figurines furnished by Mr. R. H. Capers.)

1. Animal series (from designs of Max Rüffler):
    A. Der stehende Eisbär (The Upright Polar Bear)
    B. Der hochende Bär (The crouching or squating Bear)
    C. Die Stute mit Neuling (The Mare with Colt)
    D. Der Steinbock (The Ibex)
    E. Der Windhund (The Greyhound/Whippet)

2. Character Figures from Literature:
    A. Max und Moritz (Wilhelm Busch)
    B. Die fromme Helene (The Pious Helene) (Wilhelm Busch)
    C. Die sitzende Lauterspielerin (Lady Sitting and Playing the Lute) (Wilhelm Busch -?-)
    D. Der sitzende Mandolinspieler (Man Sitting and Playing the Mandolin) (Wilhelm Busch)
    E. Die Tänzerin (The Ballerina – classic pirouette pose)
    F. Das sitzende Mädchen mit Dackel (The Sitting Girl with Dachshund)
    G. Die halbliegende Dame mit Papagei auf ihrem Knie (The Reclining Lady with a Parrot on Her Knee)
    H. Die hochende Knabenfigur mit Aschenschale auf den gebeugten Beinen (Crouching Youth with Ash Bucket on/in His Lap)
    I. Madonna (Virgin Mary)

3. Figures Based on Famous Paintings
    A. Die Badenixe (The Bathing Nymph – nude)
    B. Das Engel (The Angel)
    C. Das betende Mädchen (The Praying Girl)
    D. Liebespaar beim Frühstück (Lovers at Breakfast) by Elisabeth Jacobs Bas
    E. Der lachende junge Mann (The Laughing Young Man) by Senster
    F. Der Raucher (The Smoker) by Brouver
    G. Der Melonenesser (The Melon Eater) by Murillo
    H. Die Würfelspielern (The Dice Throwers) by Murillo
    I. Die Nachtwachegruppe (The Night Watchmen) by Rembrandt

R.S. Tillowitz Mark 2. This mark is found on the "Ibex" and the "Man Sitting and Playing the Mandolin."

The Ibex, 8"l, 6"h, 3"w.

Another view of the preceding figurine.

The Praying Girl, 4⅞"h, 2⅛"d at base.

The Man Sitting and Playing the Mandolin, 4⅞"h.

Mark on The Praying Girl. The R.S. Tillowitz Wreath Mark is accompanied by another mark which may have some religious significance.

271

Matthes and Ebel Factory

A few examples of china produced by the Matthes and Ebel factory are shown in the following photographs. This factory was the successor to the Carl Schlegelmilch factory in Mäbendorf, a suburb of Suhl. Three variations of the mark used by Matthes and Ebel are shown along with an example of a cup and saucer. The marks are in the form of an arm with a sword printed inside an oval shape. "Mäbendorf 1882" (founding date of the Carl Schlegelmilch factory) is printed around the inner edge of the oval shape. The first mark includes "reinhandgemalt" (entirely handpainted). The marks are printed in black and are overglaze. The shape and decoration of the cups and saucers are in the Art Deco style, reflecting the period of the marks, circa the 1920s through the 1930s.

Photographs and information furnished by Ms. Edda Biesterfeld of Bonn, Germany.

Erdmann Schlegelmilch Family Tree*

(Underscored names indicate line of family ownership of ES Factory)

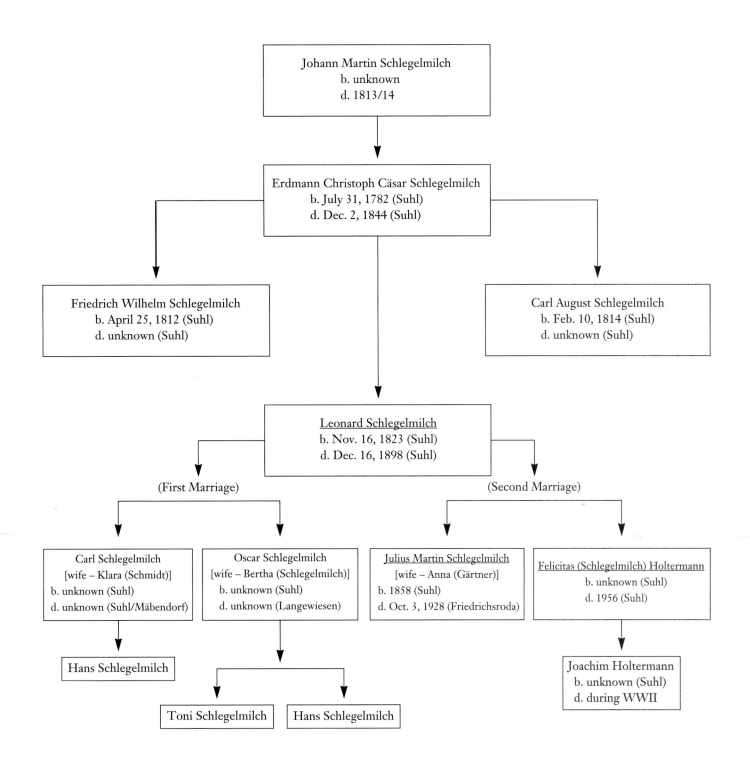

*The Erdmann Schlegelmilch Family Tree was compiled by Mr. R. H. Capers as of November 17, 1992, based on information in the Hartwich (1984) manuscript, available death notices, and church records. Minor revisions may be necessary if new information is discovered.

Death Notices for Julius Schlegelmilch

These notices are from newspapers published after the death of Julius Schlegelmilch on October 3, 1928. The first announcement was placed by his wife, Anna, for the family. The second notice was placed by factory officials of the Erdmann Schlegelmilch factory. (Copies furnished by R. H. Capers.)

Statt besonderer Anzeige.

Mittwoch abend entschlief sanft nach langem, mit Geduld getragenem Leiden mein innigstgeliebter, guter Mann, der

Fabrikbesitzer

Julius Schlegelmilch

im 70. Lebensjahre.

Anna Schlegelmilch
geb. Gärtner.

Friedrichroda, den 6. Oktober 1928.

Die Einäscherung ist nach dem Wunsche des Entschlafenen in aller Stille erfolgt.

Nachruf.

Nach langem Leiden wurde uns am 3. d. Mts. unser hochverehrter Chef,

Herr Fabrikbesitzer

Julius Schlegelmilch

in Friedrichroda durch den Tod entrissen.

In dem Heimgegangenen betrauern wir das Vorbild eines geraden, aufrichtigen Charakters, vereint mit Treue und Güte, dessen ganzes Lebenswerk dem Gedeihen seines Unternehmens und dem Wohl seiner Mitarbeiter gewidmet war.

Die Treue, die er uns im Leben gehalten, werden wir ihm über den Tod hinaus bewahren.

Die Beamten der Firma Erdmann Schlegelmilch.

Suhl, den 8. Oktober 1928.

Erdmann Schlegelmilch Factory Documents

Copies of two letterheads from the E.S. Factory: the first shows that the ES cursive monogram mark with bird was included as an insignia for the factory in 1895; the second document shows a view of the factory in 1897. It is interesting to note that these letterheads have a notation requesting that all correspondence to the factory be addressed by including the first name "Erdmann" in order to avoid confusion with other existing firms with the name "Schlegelmilch." (Factory Documents and translation furnished by R. H. Capers.)

Indexes
R.S. Prussia Mold Revisions
R.S. Steeple Floral Decorations
Other R.S. Marks Decoration Themes
Other R.S. Marks Objects
E.S. Decoration Themes
E.S. Objects
O.S. Decoration Themes
O.S. Objects
Ambiguous Marks Floral Decorations
Ambiguous Marks Decoration Themes
Ambiguous Marks Objects

R.S. Prussia Mold Revisions

RSP Mold Numbers in G1, G2, or G3	Revisions and Cross References for G3 & G4
RSP Molds 4 & 5 (Hidden Image)	Deleted, see under Ambiguous Marks, Plates 444, 449, 463 – 474
RSP Mold 6 (Hidden House)	Changed to R.S. Steeple Mold 24, see Plate 86
RSP Mold 11 (Leaf Wreath)	Deleted
RSP Mold 12a (Lettuce/Cabbage)	also see under R.S. Germany, Plates 201, 202, 310
RSP Mold 23 (Stippled Floral)	also see under R.S. Steeple Marks, Plates 144 – 148
RSP Mold 25 (Iris)	also see under R.S. Germany Marks, Plate 190
RSP Mold 25a (Iris Variation)	also see under R.S. Germany Marks, Plate 191
RSP Mold 25b (Iris Variation)	also see under Ambiguous Marks, Plate 557
RSP Molds 26 & 27 (Iris Variation)	Changed to R.S. Steeple Mold 6, see Plates 48 – 50, 103 – 115; also see under Ambiguous Marks, Plate 554
RSP Mold 28 (Carnation)	also see under R.S. Germany Marks, Plate 192
RSP Molds 29 & 30 (Lily)	also see under R. S. Steeple Marks, Plates 149 – 152; also see under Ambiguous Marks, Plate 551
RSP Mold 40 (Tulip and Ribbon)	also see under Molded R.S. Marks, Plate 423; also see under Ambiguous Marks, Plate 539
RSP Molds 51 & 52	Changed to R.S. Steeple Mold 26, see Plates 139 – 143
RSP Mold 54	Deleted
RSP Mold 86	Changed to R.S. Steeple Mold 5, see Plates 47, 100 – 102
RSP Mold 87	also see under R. S. Steeple Marks, Plate 158
RSP Mold 93	also see under R. S. Suhl Marks, Plate 38
RSP Mold 98	also see under R. S. Steeple Marks, Plates 159 – 163; also see under Ambiguous Marks, Plate 561
RSP Mold 181	also see under R. S. Suhl Marks, Plates 1, 2; also see under R. S. Tillowitz Marks, Plates 366 – 368
RSP Mold 183	also see under R. S. Germany Marks, Plate 193
RSP Mold 205	also see under R. S. Germany Marks, Plates 194, 195
RSP Mold 208	also see under R. S. Germany Marks, Plate 196
RSP Mold 256	also see under R. S. Germany Marks, Plates 197 – 199; also see under R. S. Germany Double Marks, Plate 425; also see under Ambiguous Marks, Plate 555
RSP Mold 328	Changed to Steeple Mold 1, see Plates 43, 95, 96
RSP Mold 339	also see under R. S. Steeple Marks, Plates 164, 165
RSP Mold 343	This Mold is considered as an RSP Mold when it is RSP marked and/or has an RSP decoration; it is also R.S. Steeple Mold 8 if it has a Steeple Mark and/or Steeple decoration, see Plates 62 – 65; 119 – 122; also see under R.S. Germany Marks, Plate 200; also see under Ambiguous Marks, Plates 445, 448, 450, 460 – 462, 485, 486, 493 – 496, 502, 503, 506, 507, 509, 549, 550, 562
RSP Mold 347	also see under R. S. Steeple Marks, Plate 166; also see under Ambiguous Marks, Plates 544, 547
RSP Mold 401	Deleted
RSP Mold 402	Changed to R.S. Steeple Mold 9, see Plates 66, 123
RSP Mold 462	also see under R. S. Germany Marks, Plate 323

R.S. Steeple Floral Decorations

FD Letter	Description of Pattern	Examples (by Plate Number)
A	1 pink rose with 2 yellow roses, a pink bud, and 2 yellow buds	43, 106, 117, 145, 148, 156, 164, 165, 170
B	multicolored mums	44, 102, 532
C	large white flowers with large green leaves	45, 54, 62, 63, 73, 107, 120, 175, 181, 450, 462
D	small blue and white wild flowers on long branches	46, 166
E	1 white and 2 red tulips	47, 126, 132, 133, 141, 182
F	cluster of small multicolored roses	48, 57, 58, 98, 112, 131, 191
G	large orange poppies with white flowers	48, 51, 101, 109, 183
H	a large white poppy and a large pink-orange poppy with small white flowers	49, 50, 75, 99, 103, 104, 126, 141, 142
I	poppies in shades of lavender or different colors	52, 70, 119, 128, 130, 140, 186, 502, 522
J	cluster of mixed white flowers with green leaves	53, 64
K	bouquet of pink roses, white daisies, and blue asters	55, 56, 108, 114, 176, 269
L	white flowers with a pink tint outlined in gold with large slender green leaves	59, 66, 67, 72
M	floral design painted in blue, shading from light to cobalt	68, 86, 88 – 91
N	cluster of small pink roses	65, 74, 100, 115, 125, 137, 152 – 155, 160, 180
O	small white flowers and large leaves outlined in gold	69, 82
P	floral design painted in shades of cobalt blue with light gold stems behind design	83 – 85
Q	a pink, a white, and a yellow mum	35, 71, 87, 469 – 474, 495, 538, 549
R	a large yellow flower with smaller pink, blue, and white flowers	97, 110, 138, 158, 448, 496
S	3 large yellow roses	95, 116, 144, 146, 147, 149, 151, 157, 159, 172 – 174, 551, 558, 562
T	spray of multicolored flowers with green leaves	96, 150, 161, 168, 171, 177
U	large yellow-gold roses with smaller pink roses	105, 113, 123, 127, 136, 141, 487, 514, 518
V	2 large pink roses with or without a watered silk finish	118, 124, 146, 147, 152
W	large white flowers outlined in gold	72, 134, 135, 146, 147
X	large white water lilies outlined in gold	139, 536

Other R.S. Marks Decoration Themes
by Plate Number

Other R.S. Marks Objects
by Plate Number

Other R.S. Marks Objects
(continued)

E.S. Decoration Themes
by Plate Number

E.S. Objects
by Plate Number

O.S. Decoration Themes
by Plate Number

O.S. Objects
by Plate Number

Ambiguous Marks Floral Decorations

Embossed Star FD Letter	Description of Pattern	Examples (by Plate Number)
a	a pink, a yellow, and a white mum	34, 444, 461, 464, 465, 480, 481, 485 – 488, 566
b	a cluster of small multicolored flowers	445, 466, 467
c	a cluster of yellow and pink roses	337, 446, 460, 482, 483, 503
d	3 white asters	447, 476 – 479, 484
e	gold stencilled floral pattern	454
f	variation of FDe	455
g	gold enameled flowers with red-orange center	456
h	small yellow and lavender flowers	457
i	small yellow and orange flowers	458
j	2 pink roses with 1 white and 1 yellow rose	459, 475

Saxe Altenburg FD Letter	Description of Pattern	Examples (by Plate Number)
a	spray of pink and white lilies	489, 490, 498 – 502, 504
b	cluster of small orange-white flowers	491, 503
c	yellow roses with mixed flowers	492, 503
d	white and yellow jonquils outlined in gold	493, 494, 505 – 509

Ambiguous Marks Decoration Themes
by Plate Number

Ambiguous Marks Objects

Value Guide
(Identified by Plate Number)

Reinhold Schlegelmilch China

#1	$375.00 – 425.00
#2	$350.00 – 400.00
#3	$800.00 – 1000.00
#4	$600.00 – 800.00
#5	$350.00 – 450.00
#6	$350.00 – 450.00
#7	$300.00 – 400.00
#8	$325.00 – 375.00
#9 (each)	$1300.00 – 1500.00
#10	$400.00 – 450.00
#11	$350.00 – 400.00
#12	$300.00 – 350.00
#13	$350.00 – 400.00
#14 (pair)	$300.00 – 400.00
#15 (each)	$1100.00 – 1300.00
#16	$200.00 – 250.00
#17	$175.00 – 225.00
#18	$200.00 – 250.00
#19	$200.00 – 250.00
#20	$400.00 – 500.00
#21	$175.00 – 225.00
#22 (set)	$100.00 – 125.00
#23 (set)	$80.00 – 100.00
#24	$80.00 – 100.00
#25	$140.00 – 160.00
#26	$120.00 – 140.00
#27	$150.00 – 200.00
#28	$125.00 – 175.00
#29	$1000.00 – 1200.00
#30	$1000.00 – 1200.00
#31	$1000.00 – 1200.00
#32 (each)	$800.00 – 1000.00
#33	$100.00 – 125.00
#34	$600.00 – 700.00
#35	$600.00 – 700.00
#36 (each)	$3000.00 – 3500.00
#37	see plate 36
#38	$225.00 – 275.00
#39 (set)	$1000.00 – 1200.00
#40	$3500.00 – 4000.00
#41	$1500.00 – 2000.00
#42	$4000.00 – 4500.00
#43	$175.00 – 225.00
#44	$200.00 – 250.00
#45	$150.00 – 200.00
#46	$225.00 – 275.00
#47	$140.00 – 160.00
#48 (set)	$400.00 – 500.00
#49	$200.00 – 250.00
#50	$800.00 – 1000.00
#51	$120.00 – 140.00
#52	$600.00 – 700.00
#53	$250.00 – 300.00
#54	$225.00 – 275.00
#55	$250.00 – 300.00
#56	$400.00 – 500.00
#57	$80.00 – 100.00
#58	$80.00 – 100.00
#59	$150.00 – 175.00
#60	$1200.00 – 1400.00
#61	$1400.00 – 1600.00
#62	$225.00 – 275.00
#63	$200.00 – 250.00
#64	$250.00 – 300.00
#65	$350.00 – 450.00
#66	$250.00 – 300.00
#67	$250.00 – 300.00
#68	$250.00 – 300.00
#69	$275.00 – 325.00
#70 (Pot)	$550.00 – 600.00
(Sugar/Creamer Set)	$300.00 – 400.00
#71	$350.00 – 450.00
#72 (Cracker Jar)	$225.00 – 275.00
(Sugar/Creamer Set)	$250.00 – 300.00
#73	$300.00 – 350.00
#74	$450.00 – 550.00
#75	$120.00 – 140.00
#76	$450.00 – 550.00
#77	$2500.00 – 3000.00
#78	$1400.00 – 1600.00
#79	$1400.00 – 1600.00
#80	$1200.00 – 1400.00
#81	see Plate 80
#82	$225.00 – 275.00
#83	$275.00 – 325.00
#84	$225.00 – 275.00
#85	$200.00 – 250.00
#86	$400.00 – 500.00
#87	$325.00 – 375.00
#88	$75.00 – 100.00
#89	$140.00 – 160.00
#90	$650.00 – 750.00
#91	$175.00 – 225.00
#92	$120.00 – 140.00
#93	$1300.00 – 1500.00
#94	see Plate 93
#95	$150.00 – 200.00
#96	$175.00 – 225.00
#97	$175.00 – 225.00
#98	$150.00 – 200.00
#99	$225.00 – 275.00
#100	$300.00 – 350.00
#101	$175.00 – 225.00
#102	$120.00 – 140.00
#103	$250.00 – 300.00
#104	$250.00 – 300.00
#105	$40.00 – 50.00
#106	$200.00 – 250.00
#107	$325.00 – 375.00
#108	$250.00 – 300.00
#109	$275.00 – 325.00
#110	$225.00 – 275.00
#111	$350.00 – 400.00
#112	$350.00 – 450.00
#113	$300.00 – 400.00
#114	$350.00 – 400.00
#115	$500.00 – 600.00
#116	$175.00 – 225.00
#117	$300.00 – 400.00
#118 (Pot)	$350.00 – 450.00
(Cup and Saucer)	$80.00 – 100.00
#119	$175.00 – 225.00
#120	$225.00 – 275.00
#121	$1000.00 – 1200.00
#122	$1200.00 – 1400.00
#123	$225.00 – 275.00
#124	$150.00 – 200.00
#125	$200.00 – 250.00
#126 (set)	$250.00 – 300.00
#127	$275.00 – 325.00
#128 (Pot)	$300.00 – 350.00
(Sugar/Creamer Set)	$275.00 – 325.00
#129	$700.00 – 900.00
#130	$550.00 – 650.00
#131	$500.00 – 600.00
#132 (Pot)	$450.00 – 550.00
(Cup & Saucer, ea. set)	$80.00 – 100.00
#133	$80.00 – 100.00
#134 (set)	$550.00 – 650.00
#135	$300.00 – 350.00
#136	$300.00 – 400.00
#137 (Sugar)	$140.00 – 160.00
(Teapot)	$450.00 – 550.00
#138	$175.00 – 225.00
#139	$225.00 – 250.00
#140	$150.00 – 175.00
#141 (Pot)	$200.00 – 250.00
(Sugar/Creamer Set)	$200.00 – 300.00
#142	$150.00 – 200.00
#143	$1400.00 – 1600.00
#144	$225.00 – 275.00
#145	$550.00 – 650.00
#146	$400.00 – 500.00
#147 (Pot)	$500.00 – 600.00
(Cup & Saucer, ea. set)	$100.00 – 125.00
#148 (Pot)	$550.00 – 650.00
(Cup & Saucer, ea. set)	$120.00 – 140.00
#149	$30.00 – 40.00
#150	$160.00 – 180.00

#151.....................$300.00 – 350.00
#152.....................$350.00 – 400.00
#153.............(Pot) $225.00 – 275.00
　(Sugar/Creamer Set) $250.00 – 300.00
#154.....................$350.00 – 450.00
#155.....................$75.00 – 100.00
#156.....................$400.00 – 500.00
#157.....................$450.00 – 550.00
#158.....................$140.00 – 160.00
#159.....................$275.00 – 325.00
#160.....................$100.00 – 125.00
#161.....................$175.00 – 225.00
#162.............(set) $1200.00 – 1400.00
#163.....................$1200.00 – 1400.00
#164.....................$225.00 – 275.00
#165.....................$250.00 – 300.00
#166.....................$275.00 – 325.00
#167.....................$200.00 – 250.00
#168.............(Pot) $225.00 – 275.00
　(Sugar/Creamer Set) $225.00 – 275.00
#169.............(Pot) $500.00 – 600.00
　(Sugar/Creamer Set) $400.00 – 500.00
#170.....................$200.00 – 250.00
#171.....................$450.00 – 550.00
#172.....................$500.00 – 600.00
#173.....................$325.00 – 375.00
#174.....................$250.00 – 300.00
#175.....................$275.00 – 325.00
#176.....................$250.00 – 300.00
#177.....................$450.00 – 550.00
#178.....................$500.00 – 600.00
#179.....................$1200.00 – 1400.00
#180.....................$225.00 – 275.00
#181.....................$250.00 – 300.00
#182.....................$225.00 – 275.00
#183.....................$275.00 – 325.00
#184.....................$400.00 – 500.00
#185.....................$2500.00 – 3000.00
#186.....................$375.00 – 475.00
#187.....................$150.00 – 200.00
#188.....................$175.00 – 225.00
#189.....................$175.00 – 225.00
#190.....................$1600.00 – 1800.00
#191.....................$200.00 – 250.00
#192.....................$160.00 – 185.00
#193.....................$150.00 – 175.00
#194.....................$175.00 – 200.00
#195.............(set) $300.00 – 400.00
#196.............(each) $20.00 – 30.00
#197.....................$50.00 – 60.00
#198.....................$12.00 – 15.00
#199.......(Berry Bowl) $15.00 – 20.00
　(Plate) ....$15.00 – 20.00
#200.....................$75.00 – 100.00
#201.....................$300.00 – 400.00
#202.....................$140.00 – 165.00
#203.....................$225.00 – 275.00
#204.....................$250.00 – 300.00

#205.....................$175.00 – 225.00
#206.............(left) $150.00 – 200.00
　(right) ....$175.00 – 225.00
#207.....................$175.00 – 225.00
#208.....................$40.00 – 50.00
#209.....................$60.00 – 75.00
#210.....................$50.00 – 60.00
#211.....................$50.00 – 65.00
#212.....................$20.00 – 25.00
#213.....................$70.00 – 85.00
#214.....................$50.00 – 70.00
#215.....................$45.00 – 55.00
#216.....................$80.00 – 100.00
#217.....................$20.00 – 25.00
#218.....................$50.00 – 70.00
#219.....................$60.00 – 80.00
#220.....................$25.00 – 35.00
#221.....................$75.00 – 95.00
#222.............(set) $120.00 – 140.00
#223.....................$30.00 – 40.00
#224.....................$35.00 – 45.00
#225.....................$70.00 – 90.00
#226.....................$25.00 – 35.00
#227.....................$100.00 – 120.00
#228.....................$40.00 – 50.00
#229.....................$40.00 – 50.00
#230.....................$60.00 – 75.00
#231.....................$50.00 – 65.00
#232.............(Bowl) $55.00 – 65.00
　(Individual Bowl) ....$25.00 – 30.00
#233.....................$50.00 – 60.00
#234.....................$50.00 – 65.00
#235.....................$50.00 – 70.00
#236.....................$35.00 – 45.00
#237.....................$60.00 – 75.00
#238.....................$40.00 – 50.00
#239. ....(Master Bowl) $60.00 – 70.00
　(Individual Bowl).......$25.00 – 30.00
#240.....................$35.00 – 45.00
#241.....................$20.00 – 25.00
#242.....................$70.00 – 90.00
#243........(Cake Plate) $60.00 – 70.00
　(Individual Plate)...... $25.00 – 30.00
#244.....................$50.00 – 70.00
#245.....................$50.00 – 60.00
#246.....................$65.00 – 85.00
#247.....................$70.00 – 90.00
#248.....................$45.00 – 55.00
#249.....................$70.00 – 90.00
#250.....................$35.00 – 45.00
#251.....................$20.00 – 25.00
#252.....................$60.00 – 75.00
#253.....................$65.00 – 75.00
#254.....................$40.00 – 50.00
#255.....................$15.00 – 18.00
#256.....................$40.00 – 50.00
#257.....................$50.00 – 65.00
#258.....................$60.00 – 75.00

#259.....................$50.00 – 65.00
#260.....................$70.00 – 90.00
#261.....................$75.00 – 95.00
#262.....................$60.00 – 75.00
#263........(Cake Plate) $60.00 – 70.00
　(Individual Plate)........$25.00 – 30.00
#264................(set) $60.00 – 80.00
#265.....................$80.00 – 100.00
#266.....................$70.00 – 80.00
#267.....................$70.00 – 80.00
#268.....................$65.00 – 75.00
#269.....................$60.00 – 80.00
#270.....................$150.00 – 175.00
#271.....................$70.00 – 90.00
#272.....................$15.00 – 20.00
#273.....................$25.00 – 35.00
#274.....................$100.00 – 125.00
#275.....................$75.00 – 90.00
#276........(Cake Plate) $45.00 – 55.00
　(Individual Plate).......$20.00 – 25.00
#277.....................$100.00 – 125.00
#278.....................$20.00 – 30.00
#279.....................$25.00 – 35.00
#280.....................$50.00 – 60.00
#281.....................$120.00 – 140.00
#282.....................$100.00 – 120.00
#283.....................$150.00 – 200.00
#284.....................$125.00 – 150.00
#285.....................$125.00 – 150.00
#286.....................$125.00 – 150.00
#287.....................$100.00 – 125.00
#288.....................$60.00 – 75.00
#289.....................$60.00 – 75.00
#290.....................$100.00 – 125.00
#291.....................$125.00 – 150.00
#292.....................$225.00 – 275.00
#293.............(Pot) $250.00 – 300.00
　(Cup & Saucer, ea. set) $60.00 – 75.00
#294.....................$120.00 – 140.00
#295........(Coffee Pot) $200.00 – 250.00
　(Cake Plate) ....$60.00 – 70.00
　(Sugar/Creamer w/lid)..$100.00 – 125.00
　(Cup & Saucer, ea. set) $50.00 – 60.00
　(Shaker)...................$35.00 – 40.00
　(Jam Jar w/lid).........$60.00 – 75.00
　(Mustard Pot)...........$80.00 – 100.00
　(Individual Plate, ea.)...$25.00 – 30.00
#296.............(Pot) $200.00 – 250.00
　(Cup & Saucer, ea. set) $50.00 – 60.00
#297.....................$225.00 – 275.00
#298.............(Pot) $200.00 – 250.00
　(Cup & Saucer, ea. set) $50.00 – 60.00
#299.............(Pot) $250.00 – 300.00
　(Cup & Saucer, ea. set) $55.00 – 65.00
#300.............(Pot) $350.00 – 450.00
　(Cup & Saucer, ea. set) $100.00 – 125.00
#301.............(Pot) $200.00 – 250.00
　(Cup & Saucer, ea. set) $50.00 – 60.00

#302......................$120.00 – 140.00
#303......................$35.00 – 45.00
#304......................$125.00 – 150.00
#305......................$45.00 – 55.00
#306......................$40.00 – 50.00
#307.............(set) $100.00 – 125.00
#308.............(set) $100.00 – 125.00
#309.............(set) $100.00 – 125.00
#310.............(set) $175.00 – 200.00
#311.............(set) $80.00 – 100.00
#312.............(set) $80.00 – 100.00
#313......................$35.00 – 45.00
#314......................$35.00 – 45.00
#315......................$35.00 – 45.00
#316......................$40.00 – 50.00
#317......................$40.00 – 50.00
#318......................$65.00 – 75.00
#319......................$35.00 – 45.00
#320.............(set) $80.00 – 100.00
#321......................$30.00 – 35.00
#322......................$40.00 – 50.00
#323......................$40.00 – 50.00
#324......................$35.00 – 45.00
#325......................$35.00 – 45.00
#326.........(each set) $50.00 – 60.00
#327......................$35.00 – 45.00
#328......................$50.00 – 60.00
#329......................$275.00 – 325.00
#330......................$125.00 – 150.00
#331......................$125.00 – 150.00
#332......................$100.00 – 125.00
#333......................$100.00 – 125.00
#334......................$120.00 – 140.00
#335......................$60.00 – 75.00
#336.............(each) $80.00 – 90.00
#337......................$500.00 – 600.00
#338......................$80.00 – 100.00
#339......................$100.00 – 125.00
#340......................$75.00 – 100.00
#341......................$75.00 – 100.00
#342.............(set) $100.00 – 125.00
#343.............(each) $20.00 – 30.00
#344.............(each) $15.00 – 18.00
#345.............(each) $15.00 – 18.00
#346......................$15.00 – 18.00
#347......................$15.00 – 18.00
#348......................$125.00 – 150.00
#349......................$140.00 – 160.00
#350......................$150.00 – 175.00
#351......................$400.00 – 500.00
#352......................$125.00 – 150.00
#353.............(set) $275.00 – 325.00
#354......................$125.00 – 150.00
#355......................$150.00 – 175.00
#356......................$125.00 – 150.00
#357......................$350.00 – 450.00
#358......................$400.00 – 500.00

#359...............(pair) $150.00 – 200.00
#360......................$250.00 – 300.00
#361...............(pair) $125.00 – 150.00
#362......................$1800.00 – 2000.00
#363......................$225.00 – 275.00
#364...............(Pot) $175.00 – 200.00
(Sugar/Creamer Set) $100.00 – 125.00
#365......................$80.00 – 100.00
#366......................$225.00 – 275.00
#367......................$175.00 – 225.00
#368......................$200.00 – 250.00
#369.............(set) $150.00 – 175.00
#370.............(each) $15.00 – 18.00
#371.............(each) $12.00 – 15.00
#372......................$45.00 – 55.00
#373......................$40.00 – 50.00
#374............(Sugar) $50.00 – 60.00
(Cup & Saucer) ....$50.00 – 60.00
#375...............(Pot) $225.00 – 275.00
(Sugar/Creamer Set) $120.00 – 140.00
#376.............(each set) $55.00 – 65.00
#377......................$500.00 – 600.00
#378......................$70.00 – 90.00
#379.............(each) $15.00 – 20.00
#380....(Cup & Saucer) $45.00 – 55.00
(Plate) ....$20.00 – 25.00
#381......................$200.00 – 250.00
#382......................$60.00 – 75.00
#383....(Cup & Saucer) $45.00 – 55.00
(Plate) ....$20.00 – 25.00
#384......................$250.00 – 300.00
#385...............(pair) $200.00 – 250.00
#386......................$120.00 – 140.00
#387......................$55.00 – 65.00
#388......................$45.00 – 65.00
#389......................$50.00 – 70.00
#390......................$60.00 – 80.00
#391......................$45.00 – 55.00
#392......................$30.00 – 40.00
#393......................$40.00 – 50.00
#394......................$35.00 – 45.00
#395......................$35.00 – 45.00
#396......................$125.00 – 150.00
#397......................$50.00 – 60.00
#398.............(set) $150.00 – 175.00
#399.............(set) $150.00 – 175.00
#400......................$45.00 – 55.00
#401......................$15.00 – 20.00
#402.......(Cake Plate) $50.00 – 70.00
(Individual Plate).......$25.00 – 30.00
#403......................$40.00 – 50.00
#404......................$120.00 – 140.00
#405.......(Powder Box) $75.00 – 100.00
(Hair Receiver) ....$70.00 – 90.00
#406......................$175.00 – 225.00
#407......................$150.00 – 200.00
#408......................$80.00 – 100.00

#409......................$45.00 – 55.00
#410......................$35.00 – 45.00
#411......................$30.00 – 40.00
#412......................$150.00 – 175.00
#413......................$75.00 – 100.00
#414......................$80.00 – 100.00
#415......................$200.00 – 250.00
#416......................$150.00 – 200.00
#417.............(set) $300.00 – 350.00
#418.............(set) $300.00 – 350.00
#419......................$70.00 – 80.00
#420......................$300.00 – 350.00
#421......................$200.00 – 250.00
#422......................$200.00 – 250.00
#423......................$200.00 – 250.00
#424......................$15.00 – 20.00
#425.............(set) $175.00 – 200.00
#426......................$60.00 – 80.00
#427......................$125.00 – 150.00
#428......................$45.00 – 55.00
#429......................$50.00 – 60.00
#430......................$50.00 – 60.00
#431......................$60.00 – 80.00
#432......................$400.00 – 500.00
#433.............(each) $150.00 – 175.00
#434......................$400.00 – 500.00
#435.............(each) $1300.00 – 1500.00
#436...............(pair) $250.00 – 350.00
#437......................$200.00 – 250.00
#438......................$500.00 – 600.00
#439......................$400.00 – 500.00
#440......................$400.00 – 500.00
#441......................$800.00 – 1000.00
#442......................$500.00 – 600.00
#443.............(set) $300.00 – 350.00

Ambiguous Marks China

#444......................$325.00 – 375.00
#445......................$60.00 – 75.00
#446......................$140.00 – 160.00
#447......................$70.00 – 80.00
#448.............(set) $150.00 – 160.00
#449......................$325.00 – 375.00
#450......................$175.00 – 225.00
#451......................$200.00 – 250.00
#452......................$300.00 – 350.00
#453......................$300.00 – 350.00
#454......................$75.00 – 90.00
#455......................$75.00 – 90.00
#456......................$25.00 – 35.00
#457.............(set) $80.00 – 100.00
#458..........(Sugar) $40.00 – 50.00
(Teapot)..............$75.00 – 100.00
#459......................$40.00 – 50.00
#460......................$50.00 – 65.00
#461.........(Creamer) $40.00 – 50.00

(Teapot) ....$100.00 – 125.00
#462.................$150.00 – 175.00
#463.................$500.00 – 600.00
#464.................$225.00 – 275.00
#465.................$500.00 – 600.00
#466.................$500.00 – 600.00
#467.................$550.00 – 650.00
#468.................$1200.00 – 1400.00
#469.................$350.00 – 450.00
#470.................$550.00 – 650.00
#471.................$225.00 – 275.00
#472.................$600.00 – 700.00
#473.................$450.00 – 550.00
#474.................$1000.00 – 1200.00
#475.................(set) $225.00 – 275.00
#476.................$25.00 – 35.00
#477.................$75.00 – 90.00
#478.................$60.00 – 75.00
#479.........(with lid) $150.00 – 175.00
#480.................$325.00 – 375.00
#481.................$250.00 – 300.00
#482.................$250.00 – 300.00
#483.................$120.00 – 140.00
#484.................$150.00 – 200.00
#485.................$175.00 – 225.00
#486.................$75.00 – 95.00
#487.............(Pot) $500.00 – 600.00
(Sugar/Creamer Set) $250.00 – 300.00
#488.............(each) $80.00 – 100.00
#489.................$120.00 – 140.00
#490.................$300.00 – 350.00
#491.................$400.00 – 500.00
#492.................$175.00 – 200.00
#493.................$275.00 – 325.00
#494.................$250.00 – 300.00
#495.................$45.00 – 55.00
#496.................$300.00 – 350.00
#497.................$600.00 – 700.00
#498.................$125.00 – 150.00
#499.................$150.00 – 175.00
#500.................$70.00 – 90.00
#501.................$20.00 – 30.00
#502.................$75.00 – 95.00
#503.................$80.00 – 100.00
#504.................$120.00 – 140.00
#505.................$275.00 – 325.00
#506.................$175.00 – 200.00
#507.................$200.00 – 250.00
#508.................$325.00 – 375.00
#509.................$275.00 – 325.00
#510.................$1400.00 – 1600.00
#511.................$1400.00 – 1600.00
#512.................$600.00 – 700.00
#513.................$1200.00 – 1400.00
#514.............(left) $500.00 – 600.00
(right) ....$300.00 – 400.00
#515.................$1300.00 – 1500.00

#516.................$1400.00 – 1600.00
#517.................$1200.00 – 1400.00
#518.................$1000.00 – 1200.00
#519.................$1400.00 – 1600.00
#520.................see Plate 519
#521.................$1200.00 – 1400.00
#522.................$800.00 – 1000.00
#523.................$300.00 – 350.00
#524.................$1200.00 – 1400.00
#525.................$1200.00 – 1400.00
#526.................$1200.00 – 1400.00
#527.................see Plate 526
#528.................$1000.00 – 1200.00
#529.................$1000.00 – 1200.00
#530.................$1300.00 – 1500.00
#531.................$1300.00 – 1500.00
#532.................$400.00 – 500.00
#533.................$1400.00 – 1600.00
#534.................$1000.00 – 1200.00
#535.................$600.00 – 800.00
#536.................$175.00 – 225.00
#537.................$800.00 – 1000.00
#538.................$125.00 – 150.00
#539.................$75.00 – 100.00
#540.................$65.00 – 75.00
#541.................$400.00 – 500.00
#542.................$900.00 – 1100.00
#543.................$800.00 – 1000.00
#544.................$140.00 – 160.00
#545.................$225.00 – 275.00
#546.................$150.00 – 175.00
#547.................$175.00 – 225.00
#548.................$400.00 – 500.00
#549.................$75.00 – 100.00
#550.............(set) $800.00 – 1000.00
#551.................$20.00 – 25.00
#552.................$70.00 – 90.00
#553.................$700.00 – 900.00
#554.................$200.00 – 250.00
#555.................$20.00 – 25.00
#556.................$125.00 – 150.00
#557.................$600.00 – 700.00
#558.................$450.00 – 550.00
#559.............(set) $150.00 – 175.00
#560.................$70.00 – 80.00
#561.................$175.00 – 225.00
#562.................$225.00 – 275.00
#563.............(set) $120.00 – 140.00
#564.................$275.00 – 325.00
#565.................$35.00 – 45.00

Children's China and Novelties

#566........(set for 6) $1200.00 – 1400.00
#567........(set for 4) $1600.00 – 1800.00
#568.........(set for 1) $800.00 – 1000.00
#569.........(set for 2) $500.00 – 700.00

#570........(set for 6) $1200.00 – 1400.00
#571..........(set for 2) $300.00 – 400.00
#572.................$75.00 – 100.00
#573.............(each set) $50.00 – 60.00
#574.................$150.00 – 175.00
#575.................$75.00 – 100.00
#576. ....(Bell) $125.00 – 150.00
(Cup) ....$70.00 – 80.00
#577. ....(Bell) $125.00 – 150.00
(Cup) ....$75.00 – 95.00

Erdmann Schlegelmilch China

#578.................$150.00 – 175.00
#579.................$150.00 – 175.00
#580.................$60.00 – 70.00
#581.................$50.00 – 60.00
#582.................$40.00 – 50.00
#583.................$450.00 – 550.00
#584.................$300.00 – 400.00
#585.................$275.00 – 325.00
#586.................$200.00 – 250.00
#587.................$75.00 – 100.00
#588.................$125.00 – 150.00
#589.................$125.00 – 150.00
#590.................$325.00 – 375.00
#591.................$350.00 – 450.00
#592.................$200.00 – 250.00
#593.................$250.00 – 300.00
#594.................$250.00 – 300.00
#595.................$150.00 – 200.00
#596.................$175.00 – 225.00
#597.............(set) $250.00 – 350.00
#598.................$350.00 – 450.00
#599.................$350.00 – 450.00
#600.................$350.00 – 450.00
#601.............(set) $225.00 – 275.00
#602.................$75.00 – 100.00
#603.................$225.00 – 275.00
#604.................$200.00 – 250.00
#605.................$140.00 – 160.00
#606.................$75.00 – 100.00
#607.................$200.00 – 250.00
#608.................$300.00 – 400.00
#609.................$200.00 – 300.00
#610.................$150.00 – 175.00
#611.................$300.00 – 400.00
#612.................$200.00 – 250.00
#613.................$200.00 – 300.00
#614.................$275.00 – 325.00
#615.................$200.00 – 300.00
#616.................$200.00 – 300.00
#617.................$250.00 – 350.00
#618.................$300.00 – 400.00
#619.................$400.00 – 500.00
#620.................$600.00 – 800.00
#621.................$600.00 – 800.00

#622	$600.00 – 800.00
#623	$250.00 – 350.00
#624	$400.00 – 500.00
#625 (each)	$200.00 – 300.00
#626	$250.00 – 350.00
#627	$275.00 – 325.00
#628	$150.00 – 200.00
#629	$150.00 – 175.00
#630	$150.00 – 175.00
#631	$500.00 – 600.00
#632	see Plate 631
#633	$200.00 – 250.00
#634	$225.00 – 275.00
#635	$125.00 – 150.00
#636	$125.00 – 150.00
#637	$150.00 – 175.00
#638	$120.00 – 140.00
#639	$20.00 – 30.00
#640	$60.00 – 75.00
#641	$20.00 – 30.00
#642	$70.00 – 80.00
#643	$15.00 – 20.00
#644	$60.00 – 75.00
#645 (set)	$55.00 – 65.00
#646 (set)	$35.00 – 45.00
#647	$30.00 – 40.00
#648 (set)	$60.00 – 70.00
#649 (Sugar/Creamer Set)	$80.00 – 100.00
(Vase)	$75.00 – 85.00
(Salt/Pepper Shakers)	$60.00 – 80.00
(Toothpick Holder)	$75.00 – 100.00
#650	$300.00 – 400.00
#651 (Pot)	$225.00 – 275.00
(Cup & Saucer, ea. set)	$45.00 – 55.00
#652	$300.00 – 400.00
#653	$50.00 – 65.00
#654	$100.00 – 125.00
#655	$175.00 – 200.00
#656	$175.00 – 200.00
#657	$65.00 – 75.00
#658	$500.00 – 600.00
#659	$350.00 – 450.00
#660	$400.00 – 500.00
#661	$550.00 – 650.00
#662	$450.00 – 550.00
#663	$500.00 – 600.00
#664 (pair)	$2000.00 – 2500.00
#665	$300.00 – 400.00
#666	$1100.00 – 1300.00
#667	see Plate 666
#668	$500.00 – 600.00
#669	$600.00 – 700.00
#670	$250.00 – 300.00
#671	$650.00 – 750.00
#672	$300.00 – 400.00
#673	$160.00 – 180.00
#674	$140.00 – 160.00

#675 (pair)	$225.00 – 250.00
#676	$140.00 – 160.00
#677	$160.00 – 180.00
#678	$120.00 – 140.00
#679 (each set)	$150.00 – 175.00
#680	$120.00 – 140.00
#681	$120.00 – 140.00
#682	$55.00 – 65.00
#683	$55.00 – 65.00
#684	$250.00 – 350.00
#685	$350.00 – 450.00
#686	$450.00 – 550.00
#687	$250.00 – 350.00
#688	$275.00 – 375.00
#689	$500.00 – 600.00
#690	see Plate 689
#691	$60.00 – 75.00
#692 (each)	$100.00 – 125.00
#693	$120.00 – 140.00
#694	$100.00 – 125.00
#695	$30.00 – 40.00
#696	$45.00 – 55.00
#697 (set)	$80.00 – 100.00
#698	$120.00 – 140.00
#699	$15.00 – 20.00
#700	$60.00 – 75.00
#701 (set)	$70.00 – 90.00
#702	$45.00 – 55.00
#703 (Tray)	$120.00 – 140.00
(Hair Receiver)	$60.00 – 75.00
(Powder Box)	$70.00 – 90.00
#704	$400.00 – 500.00
#705	$75.00 – 100.00
#706	$75.00 – 100.00
#707	$300.00 – 400.00
#708	$35.00 – 45.00
#709	$75.00 – 90.00
#710 (Pot)	$225.00 – 275.00
(Cup & Saucer, ea. set)	$45.00 – 55.00
#711	$15.00 – 20.00
#712	$30.00 – 35.00
#713	$75.00 – 90.00
#714 (set)	$70.00 – 90.00
#715	$50.00 – 65.00
#716	$200.00 – 250.00
#717	$400.00 – 500.00
#718	$225.00 – 275.00
#719	$225.00 – 275.00
#720	$300.00 – 400.00
#720a (center)	$300.00 – 400.00
(pair)	$200.00 – 300.00
#721	$300.00 – 350.00

Oscar Schlegelmilch China

#722 (pair)	$450.00 – 550.00
#723 (each set)	$150.00 – 175.00

#724	$250.00 – 300.00
#725 (Pot)	$400.00 – 500.00
(Cup & Saucer, ea. set)	$140.00 – 160.00
#726	$300.00 – 400.00
#727	$400.00 – 500.00
#728	$325.00 – 425.00
#729	$150.00 – 175.00
#730	$300.00 – 400.00
#731	$300.00 – 350.00
#732	$60.00 – 75.00
#733	$100.00 – 120.00
#734	$120.00 – 140.00
#735	$800.00 – 1000.00
#736	$225.00 – 325.00
#737	see Plate 736
#738	$70.00 – 90.00
#739	$80.00 – 100.00
#740	$70.00 – 90.00
#741 (Tray)	$400.00 – 500.00
(Teapot)	$350.00 – 400.00
(Sugar/Creamer Set)	$400.00 – 500.00
(Cup, each)	$140.00 – 160.00
#742	$120.00 – 140.00
#743	$120.00 – 140.00
#744 (each)	$16.00 – 20.00
#745	$120.00 – 140.00
#746	$150.00 – 175.00
#747 (each)	$225.00 – 275.00
#748	$300.00 – 400.00
#749	$200.00 – 250.00
#750 (each set)	$55.00 – 65.00
#751	$120.00 – 140.00
#752 (set)	$175.00 – 225.00
#753 (each set)	$45.00 – 55.00
#754	$70.00 – 90.00
#755	$120.00 – 140.00
#756 (each)	$60.00 – 70.00
#757 (set)	$175.00 – 225.00
#758 (each)	$60.00 – 70.00
#759 (Pot)	$175.00 – 225.00
(Sugar/Creamer Set)	$75.00 – 100.00
(Cup & Saucer, ea. set)	$40.00 – 50.00
#760 (set for 6)	$1000.00 – 1200.00
#761	$325.00 – 425.00
#762	$275.00 – 325.00
#763 (Pot)	$300.00 – 350.00
(Sugar/Creamer Set)	$225.00 – 275.00
(Cup & Saucer, ea. set)	$140.00 – 160.00

Carl Schlegelmilch China

#764 (set)	$60.00 – 75.00
#765	$35.00 – 45.00
#766	$70.00 – 85.00
#767	$35.00 – 45.00
#768	$80.00 – 90.00

288